The Colorado Pass Book

A GUIDE TO COLORADO'S BACKROAD MOUNTAIN PASSES

By Don Koch

SECOND EDITION

PRUETT **P** PUBLISHING COMPANY
Boulder, Colorado

Second Edition
2 3 4 5 6 7 8 9

Printed in the United States of America

Library of Congress Cataloging-in-Publication Data

Koch, Don, 1942-
    The Colorado pass book.

    Bibliography: p.
    Includes index.
    1. Automobiles—Road guides—Colorado.
2. Automobiles—Touring. 3. Mountain passes—
Colorado—Guide-book. 4. Colorado—Description and
travel—1981-   —Guide-books. I. Title.
GV1024.K63   1987   917.88′0433   87-16677
ISBN 0-87108-728-6

Printed in the United States of America

Acknowledgments

No man is an island unto himself and few books ever spring forth from an author's hand unaided. Any illusions I ever had to the contrary have long since vanished.

A special debt of gratitude is due my backcountry traveling companions and good friends, Glenn and Sue Kissinger, whose wisdom, judgment, patience and expertise have saved me from making and from repeating more mistakes than I care to remember. Special thanks are also due to Dick Hart. Not only do his finely crafted photographs grace several of the following pages, but he provided me with a broad range of technical advice, moral support and editorial assistance at every stage of the book's development.

This project has also benefited from the invaluable resources of the Denver Public Library and especially the ever-helpful assistance of that fine institution's Western History Department and staff. Dr. Lou Campbell, former State Cartographer, provided me with generous access to both his immaculately organized map files and his encyclopedic knowledge of things cartographic; Bob Martinez, of the Colorado Department of Local Affairs, has continued that tradition of assistance. Phil Schmuck—mountaineer, administrator and photographer—both granted me the necessary time off from more mundane matters to complete the field research for the first edition of this book and provided me with a model of photographic excellence and moral persistence in the high country. The late Gregg Chancellor of the Colorado Division of Commerce and Development kindly granted me access to his stockpile of photos and printed matter. William H.E. Davis of Pablo, Montana has generously contributed his own storehouse of hard-gained knowledge regarding Colorado's backcountry passes. Andrew Nigrini, the guru of Huerfano County, and Mark Lowery, a wizard of technical information on most every subject, have led me on a variety of southern Colorado journeys, gently correcting my misconceptions along the way.

The National Forest Service provided me with valuable maps along with invaluable advice, route-finding assistance and road condition reports. Dozens of Forest Service personnel halted their daily round of activities to answer patiently the barrage of questions I asked of them. So, too, have countless Coloradans generously offered me information, assistance and even sustenance during the course of my travels. It is a high tribute to those who visit and live in the Colorado Rockies that theft and vandalism, even of the most petty sort, are not problems that I have ever encountered during my backcountry journeys. And I am also grateful for the kind indulgence of Bonnie McAndrews, Leslie Beltromi, Kay Berenbaum and various other friends, who have occasionally accompanied me on rambling sojourns through the Colorado Rockies in search of yet another elusive road.

For continuing editorial guidance, advice and support I am indebted to my father, Norman Koch, my grandmother, Dorothy Cohen, to Tom Koch, Jerry Keenan of Pruett Publishing Company and, once again, of course, to Glenn and Sue Kissinger.

Contents

For Joanne and Jennifer and for Pilar Norman:
that they too may enjoy what man and nature have wrought.

Introduction

The early explorers of the Central Southern Rocky Mountain region, the men who traveled with Coronado, with Fathers Escalante and Dominguez, with Lewis and Clark, with Zebulon Pike, with Lieutenant John Fremont, and with the Hayden, King, and Wheeler surveys, invariably sought out the low routes that they hoped would yield relatively easy passage through a difficult and dangerous land. Though the high peaks captured their imagination and served as important points of geographic reference, it was the low saddle across a ridge or a gap between the mountain ranges that opened the way through the vast maze of drainage basins forming the Rocky Mountain landscape.

With the discovery of gold and later silver in the Colorado Rockies, the early pass trails developed by Indians and a few hardy European adventurers swiftly widened into wagon roads, stage coach routes, and, in time, railroad rights-of-way to bring supplies in and to haul ore out. The period from 1860 to 1890 brought a frenzy of road building as work crews surveyed, dug, blasted, and tunneled their way over the highest passes on the continent. Profit was the motive—profit from passenger fares, freight revenues, and new outlets for the goods and services needed to drive a booming, free-for-all frontier economy. Ironically, few of the mountain pass toll roads made a profit for long. High construction costs, massive maintenance expenses, exhausted mines, and competition from—and among—the railroads eventually pushed most of the original toll route ventures into bankruptcy and receivership. But these routes, even when short-lived, were important links tying together a mountain mining culture and joining it with the more civilized portions of a young expansive nation that knew itself bound for glory.

Some of these linear monuments to the skill and courage of the nineteenth century road builders—routes such as Berthoud Pass, Loveland Pass, Fremont Pass, and Red Mountain Pass—lived on to become household words among Colorado travelers. But dozens of other high pass roads, though still traversable, have slipped into obscurity. Where Indians, traders, trappers, miners, and desperados once roamed in an age of unbridled opportunity, only a few summertime visitors now travel. Despite the availability of relatively safe, speedy methods of backcountry travel, most tourists continue to follow a few well-beaten routes through the high country.

This situation is not so fortunate as it may seem to some people. The preservation of Colorado's historic mountain pass roads requires periodic use and a bit of maintenance in order to slow down or reverse the deterioration caused by nature. Eventually the mountains will reclaim these pathways, or man may decide to put the land they rest upon to other uses. In the meantime, however, Colorado's backcountry gateways are there to be enjoyed by this generation and to be preserved for future generations. It is to the preservation and enjoyment of these backcountry pass roads that the following pages are dedicated.

About These Pass Roads

No one agrees on exactly what a pass road is, and how many pass roads there are, or were, in Colorado. Just as many unnamed mountain peaks exist in the Colorado Rockies, so, too, are there many pass routes with no official names. Alternately, several passes are known by more than one name, and occasionally the common name for the route is different then the officially designated name. Some government maps list passes omitted on other government maps, and no map series has been updated to show all the passes formally named by the United States Board on Geographic Names. Then too, some pass roads are barely roads at all, or have deteriorated to trails on one side of the route. Other pass roads are now blocked by private land closures on one side, such as at La Salle Pass, or on both sides of the summit, such as at Whiskey Pass.

In the face of this uncertainty and confusion, few definitive answers are possible. Of the officially named passes with roads leading from at least one side to the summit, there are four such routes with a summit elevation above thirteen thousand feet, twelve such roads (including the two Engineer Mountain passes and Independence Pass) with summits above twelve thousand feet in elevation, and some additional thirty pass roads with summits in the eleven thousand foot range. Yet this listing of officially named passes far from exhausts the list of actual Colorado pass roads above eleven thousand feet in elevation, it ignores a few of the most spectacular routes, such as Black Bear Pass and, of course, it omits a vast number of lower but still very scenic routes of considerable historic interest.

For the purposes of this book, a pass is defined as an existing route, crossing or skirting a ridge or mountain range and connecting two drainage basins across a low point, gap or convenient route. Backcountry pass roads, the subject of this book, are unpaved and usually little-maintained routes that can, at least under ideal conditions, be traveled by a motor vehicle to the summit from at least one side. Nearly all of the backcountry pass roads included in this book are not cleared of snow in the winter, most do not receive much maintenance in the summer months; many are not open to travel along their full length until mid-summer, and a few remain snowbound near the summit year-round after a severe winter or heavy spring snows.

Although some of the backcountry pass roads described on the following pages cannot be crossed by a passenger car, this is not a book about jeep roads or primarily intended for four-wheel drive enthusiasts. Nearly half the routes I have included can be traveled safely from one end to the other with a passenger car, provided that the road conditions are good, the driver experienced and the vehicle reasonably small and agile.

Several additional pass roads, such as the routes to Georgia Pass, Schofield Pass, Ptarmigan Pass and Elwood Pass, require four-wheel drive on one side but many passenger cars can reach the summit from the other side. These instances are mentioned in the individual pass descriptions. Then too, the base area of many passes requiring four-wheel drive for the summit stretch is open to passenger cars and offers an excellent hiking, skiing or showshoeing ascent to the summit. And finally, single track vehicles of either the motorized kind (motorcycles) or non-motorized type (mountain bicycles) can travel through some places, such as a snowfield, that no four-wheel drive vehicle could traverse.

This book includes mention of almost every major backcountry pass road in Colorado along with many of the minor pass roads. I have, however, omitted any reference to a few such roads and made only indirect reference to many others for several reasons. First, it has not been my objective to provide a definitive guide to every pass road in Colorado. Instead, I have elected to focus the main body of this book on the more historically important routes, the more scenic routes, and the routes in closer proximity to urban areas. And rather than write a narrowly focused book about one type of backcountry road, it has been my objective to tie the emergence of this specialized road network into the history and development of Colorado.

The last two parts of this book, the Addendum and the Sampler of Additional Pass Roads, prepared for the second edition, pick up where the main body of the text leaves off, providing descriptions of some lesser known and more remote pass roads along with a few that I just plain missed the first time around. But even this enlarged second edition certainly does not include all, or even nearly all of the pass roads in Colorado. My hope is that these oversights and omissions will motivate readers to do a bit of independent research and exploration, finding their own favorite routes either ignored or given but brief mention herein.

A Word of Caution

The information in this volume was compiled from a wide variety of sources. Foremost among them was my continuing experience gathered from many miles of backcountry pass road travel by jeep, trail bike, passenger car, on foot, and even on skis. This firsthand experience was supplemented with the personal reports of other pass road travelers, historical research, secondary sources, and careful study of U.S. Geological Survey maps, aerial photographs, and film-positive orthophotoquads.

Yet no source of information or combination of sources can supply wholly accurate route information or provide wholly current road condition reports. Closures by private landowners and federal land management agencies periodically block access routes or side roads. A rock slide, avalanche, or rain storm may obliterate or reshape stretches of road. Sudden changes in weather, for which the Colorado Rockies are so justly famous, can turn a summer afternoon jaunt into a hair-raising test of a backcountry traveler's skill and courage. Even the best maps occasionally show roads that no longer exist or fail to indicate the existence of readily passable roads. Route markers often do not exist and, where present, are not always reliable. The Colorado Rockies are an environment of constant cultural and geologic change.

Moreover, the road condition reports and hazard notations included in this book are for the most part the result of trips taken under generally good weather conditions in vehicles well equipped for rough country travel. A bit of snow and ice, insufficient ground clearance, or too much track width can create hazards where none would otherwise exist. In addition, tolerance to perceived physical danger, or "exposure" as it is called by technical rock climbers, varies drastically from person to person and any individual's tolerance to it can change dramatically over time. Although there may be men and women of adventure who would enjoy a jeep trip down the Black Bear Pass road, more cautious souls will find the east side descent of Webster Pass quite harrowing enough, thank you.

The answer to these problems is certainly not to avoid the mountains or stay on the blacktop. Far from it. Adventure, beauty, and the other pleasures that the Colorado Rockies offer in such ample measure usually begin far from the asphalt ribbons laid down by the highway department. But to enjoy best these pleasures it is necessary to plan ahead, be prepared, and act sensibly. Printed below are eight cautionary suggestions for backcountry pass travelers.

- Take ample water, warm clothing, food, and other supplies (*see* Appendix B).
- Take appropriate maps and a compass to read them (*see* Appendix A).
- Check carefully the condition of your equipment before departing. Know how to use it, know its limitations and do not exceed them.
- Start early. Winter days are short and summer afternoons often stormy. Leave ample time for unanticipated problems.
- Remember that drugs and alcohol mix badly with mountain travel. They distort reality and impair judgment.
- Be careful with fire and be respectful of public and private property.
- Avoid traveling alone and do not drive off designated roadways.
- Remember that if a road or trail cannot be safely traveled, it should not be traveled at all.
- Anticipate the unexpected and you will not be unpleasantly surprised.

KEY MAP OF THE PAS

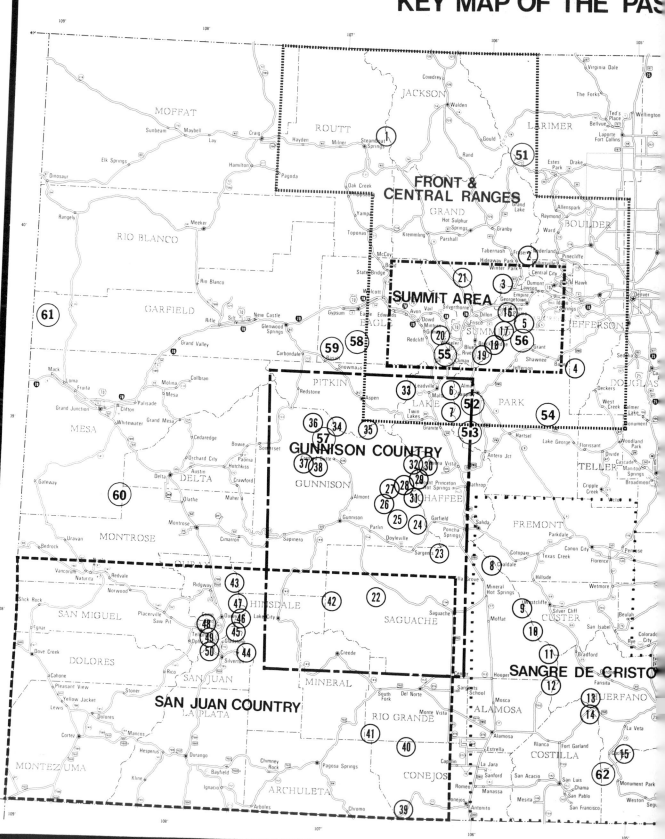

ROADS

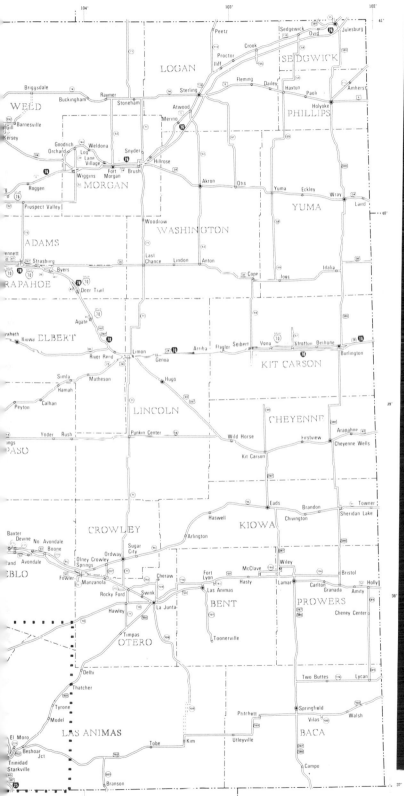

COLORADO BACKCOUNTRY PASS ROADS

1. BUFFALO
2. ROLLINS
3. JONES
4. STONEY
5. GUANELLA
6. MOSQUITO
7. WESTON
8. HAYDEN
9. HERMIT
10. MUSIC
11. MEDANO
12. MOSCA
13. PASS CREEK
14. LA VETA
15. APISHAPA
16. ARGENTINE
17. WEBSTER
18. GEORGIA
19. BOREAS
20. SHRINE
21. UTE
22. COCHETOPA
23. MARSHALL
24. OLD MONARCH
25. BLACK SAGE
26. WAUNITA
27. CUMBERLAND
28. TOMICHI
29. HANCOCK
30. WILLIAMS
31. TINCUP
32. COTTONWOOD
33. HAGERMAN
34. PEARL
35. TAYLOR
36. SCHOFIELD
37. KEBLER
38. OHIO
39. CUMBRES
40. STUNNER
41. ELWOOD
42. LOS PIÑOS
43. OWL CREEK
44. STONY
45. CINNAMON
46. NO. ENGINEER MT.
47. SO. ENGINEER MT.
48. IMOGENE
49. BLACK BEAR
50. OPHIR
51. FALL RIVER PASS
52. BROWNS AND
53. BREAKNECK PASSES
54. LA SALLE PASS
55. PTARMIGAN PASS
56. RED CONE PASS
57. GUNSIGHT PASS
58. CROOKED CREEK PASS
59. WEST COTTONWOOD PASS
60. COLUMBINE PASS
61. BAXTER PASS
62. NO NAME PASS

"In the mountains, there you feel free."
T. S. Eliot, *The Wasteland*

Converted railroad trestle on Rollins Pass road.

Front & Central Range Passes:1-7

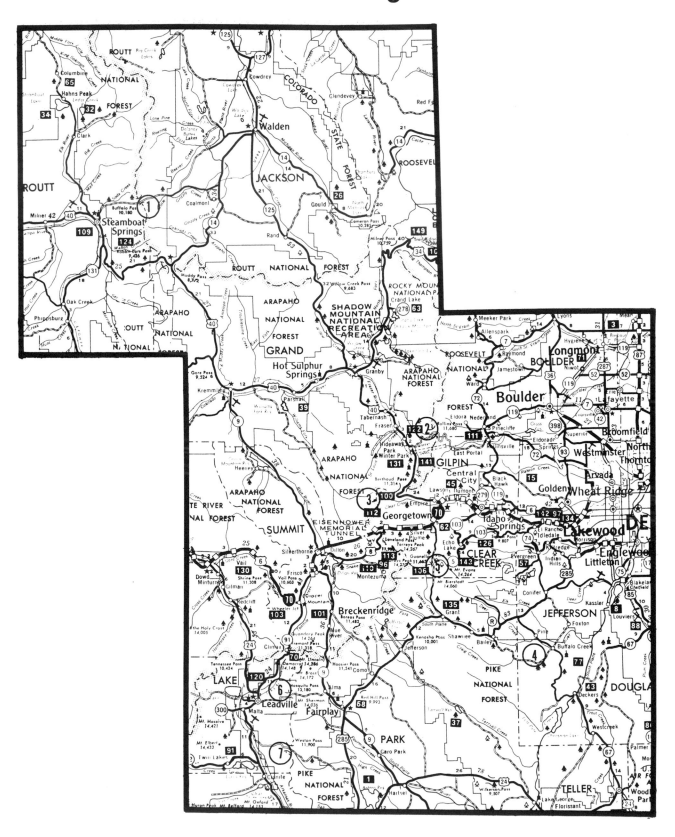

Part One
Front and Central Range Passes

Contrary to popular imagination, the Rocky Mountains are not a single spine of rock stretching 3,000 miles from Alaska to New Mexico. To be sure, it is possible to trace along the course of the Rockies a continuous line separating those drainages that flow ultimately to the Pacific from those that flow toward the Atlantic Ocean. Nevertheless, the Rockies are, in fact, a composite of greater and lesser ranges arranged in a seemingly haphazard pattern that is the result of complex geologic changes that occurred over a period of more than one billion years.

It is in Colorado that the Rockies soar to their highest elevation: more than 1,000 peaks reach above 10,000 feet, and 54 (or 53, depending on how you count them) exceed 14,000 feet. These highest peaks, the fourteeners, are concentrated in no single range; instead, they occur among one-half dozen of the major ranges in Colorado, stretching from the first large peaks that rise above the plains to the southwestern corner of the state. So, too, are Colorado's mountain pass roads widely distributed throughout the mountainous portions of Colorado. Many of these crossings are clustered in relatively compact areas such as the Sawatch Range, the San Juans, and the Sangre de Cristos. Others are scattered among a variety of front and central mountain groups such as the Park Range, the Front Range, the Platte River Mountains, the Mosquito Range, and the Gore Range. Some of these central range crossings are described separately in the sections on Summit County pass roads and the Sangre de Cristos. The remainder, which do not comprise an exhaustive catalog of backcountry pass roads through the front and central ranges, are included in this section.

The introductory sampler presented in this section includes the highest continuous pass road in Colorado—Mosquito Pass—and one of the lowest routes, namely, Stoney Pass. It also includes several better known routes such as Rollins Pass and Guanella Pass, as well as some of the more obscure backcountry pass roads, such as the crossings at Buffalo Pass and Stoney Pass. Rollins Pass is one of the longest crossings in the state; Jones Pass, also in this section, is one of the shortest routes. Mosquito Pass and the Rollins Pass route are among the most historically interesting crossings in Colorado. Stoney Pass, on the other hand, is a lovely little crossing for which I could find no historical record.

The pass roads described within this section include steep shelf roads, long traverses far above timberline, alpine meadows, a tunnel, lovely roadside lakes, fine stands of aspen, striking rock formations, and many miles of travel through little used mountain forests. This diversity of terrain is a fitting introduction to the following sections, for different settings and a variety of road conditions are two of the hallmarks that characterize Colorado's backcountry pass roads. Each of the routes described in this section has a unique character, and rarely do two trips over the same road yield the same experiences, which is the joy of backcountry travel. It is a renewable activity that never wearies the soul.

1

1 Buffalo Pass

Location: between Walden and Steamboat
    Springs
Difficulty: can be traversed by most smaller,
    high-centered passenger cars
Scenic Quality: attractive area of rolling
    woodlands
Historic Interest: modest
Side Roads: a few of interest
High Point: 10,180 feet
Maps: USFS map of Routt National Forest at
    1:125,000
USGS sheet 3 of Jackson County at 1:50,000
USGS sheet 4 of Routt County at 1:50,000
Colorado Highway map at 1:1,000,000

Today, the principal route west from the high, broad expanse of North Park travels south to the top of Muddy Pass and then west over Rabbit Ears Pass into Steamboat Springs and the Yampa Valley. But it was not always so. For

a period of several decades, until shortly after the end of World War I, the main road west out of North Park led from Walden over a slightly higher crossing than Rabbit Ears that descended from the high pine forests of the Park Range into Steamboat Springs. A state map, published by the Clason Map Company in 1919, shows the Victory Highway, now US 40, crossing over Rabbit Ears Pass on its way west to Salt Lake City. But the Buffalo Pass road is also shown as a secondary auto route from Walden to Steamboat Springs.

Present day Colorado highway maps still show the Buffalo Pass road but classify it as a graveled road about which local inquiry should be made concerning conditions. This is an apt description, because the road has become a scenic, little used byway with several rough stretches along the upper portion of the east side. The area traversed by the road is characteristic of the northern Colorado Rockies: not spectacular views and wildly rugged countryside, but a land of end-

The Yampa Valley from Buffalo Pass.

lessly rolling mountain forests dotted with small lakes and delightfully empty of the crowds that accumulate on summer weekends in the more intensively used mountain recreation areas of Colorado.

From the west side approach, the Buffalo Pass road is not easy to find. In Steamboat Springs on US Highway 40, turn north on 7th Street, following the signs to the hospital. Then take Nob Street and follow the Buffalo Pass signs to Routt County Road 38, taking this road past Bear Pole Ranch on a winding uphill ride through stands of aspen and pine that open onto pleasant views of Steamboat Springs and the Yampa Valley. After crossing a rolling meadow, the road gently climbs to a smooth, open summit and a rougher, more heavily wooded east side descent that provides excellent views of North Park as it drops from the Park Range to the quiet grazing lands below. About ten miles east of the Grizzly Creek Campground the road exits on Colorado Highway 14 at a point thirty miles from Steamboat Springs and about a dozen miles south of Walden. To approach Buffalo Pass from the east, take the road from Colorado 14 to Grizzly Creek Campground, and at the several forks along the route, follow the signs to Buffalo Pass.

Although the Park Range does not contain a well-developed road network, a few interesting side roads are in the area. From Grizzly Creek Campground, side roads travel both north and south along the flank of the range and pass a variety of small lakes. At the summit of Buffalo Pass a short route extends north to Summit Lake, and a Forest Service road extends south from the Continental Divide about four miles to Fish Creek Reservoir and Granite Campground.

A mountain scene near the summit of Buffalo Pass.

3

2 Rollins (or Corona) Pass

Location: between Rollinsville and Winter Park
Difficulty: can be traversed by most passenger
  cars under good conditions
Scenic Quality: excellent, with especially good
  views on the east side and summit area
Historic Interest: very high
Side Roads: several of interest
High Point: 11,671 feet
Maps: USFS map of Roosevelt National Forest
  at 1:125,000
USFS map of Arapaho National Forest
  at 1:125,000
USGS single sheet of Boulder County
  at 1:50,000
USGS sheet 4 of Grand County at 1:50,000
Colorado highway map at 1:1,000,000

Jenny Lake on the route to Rollins Pass.

Few roads in Colorado can boast so rich a history as the Rollins Pass route. Originally an Indian trail, it was developed as a wagon crossing in 1865 by the U.S. Army and by Mormon pioneers bound for Utah. Eight years later John Quincy Adams Rollins completed a toll road over the pass at a cost of $40,000, thereby providing a direct link between the Great Plains and Middle Park. Rollins also established the still existing town of Rollinsville (on Colorado Highway 72) to capture the commercial and tourist business that his pass route generated. During this period the route was known as Boulder Pass; it appears by that name in F. V. Hayden's 1877 *Atlas of Colorado*.

Following completion of the Berthoud Pass road, which crosses the Continental Divide about a dozen miles farther south, Rollins Pass declined in popularity. But shortly after the turn of the century, the Rollins Pass road was converted into a rail route by David Moffat, a Denver financier and mining baron who controlled the Denver, Northwestern and Pacific Railroad. The destination of Moffat's ambitiously named railroad was Salt Lake City. However, because of high construction costs and a lack of capital, the DN&P never got beyond Craig, Colorado. Although Moffat's railroad did not leave Colorado, it reached new heights: the Rollins Pass route still stands as the highest altitude ever reached by a through railroad line in the United States.

At the pass summit, the railroad constructed various service facilities, including a restaurant and workmen's bunkhouse; this service community was known as Corona (Spanish for "crest"). In fact, Clason's *Colorado Hotel Guide and Commercial Index* for 1909 identifies the pass route

by this name, not as Rollins Pass. Moffat's name was attached not to his high-altitude railroad route, but to the tunnel that replaced it. In 1927 a six-mile tunnel under the Continental Divide was built to eliminate the delays and high operating costs that plagued the pass route. Company officials once estimated that forty-one percent of the line's operating costs were devoted to snow removal. To construct the Moffat Tunnel, the Colorado legislature formed a special improvements district. At election time, Denver property owners still perform the ritual of selecting candidates to represent them on the Moffat Tunnel Commission, which governs the district.

David Moffat's railroad route over "the top of the world," as it was advertised, continued to operate sporadically until 1937, after which the line was discontinued. For nearly twenty years the Rollins Pass route fell into disuse. Then, in 1956, the railroad bed was converted into a scenic roadway and renamed Corona Pass. Fortunately, the newer name has not been well accepted. Most maps and nearly everyone who uses the route still refer to it as Rollins Pass, which is a fitting tribute to the builder of the first pass road.

Regardless of the name by which it is called, the Rollins Pass road deservedly ranks among the best known and most heavily used backcountry pass roads in Colorado. On a mild Sunday afternoon in summertime, the traffic level and the airborne dust can become bothersome. But the route is mild and very scenic. Because the Rollins Pass route, like the Boreas Pass and Marshall Pass roads, was constructed along a railway grade, it is a long but gentle road offering alpine lakes, wooden trestles, a rock tunnel, and outstanding mountain vistas.

From the east side, Rollins Pass is normally reached from State Highway 119, at Rollinsville. An improved gravel road travels west up Boulder Creek to East Portal, which is the east side mouth of the Moffat Tunnel. About a mile before the tunnel entrance, a Forest Service sign points to the "Corona Pass" road, from which point it is about fifteen miles to the summit. The east side of the road includes several narrow portions and a washboard road surface that will tax the suspension of softly sprung cars. As the road climbs, it travels in a semicircle around Yankee Doodle Lake, and then it passes beside Jenny Lake. Above this second lake is the only remaining railroad tunnel, appropriately known as the Needle's Eye. A shelf road (though not so fearsome as the shelf roads on Pearl Pass or Webster Pass) continues to the twin trestles that traverse the Devil's Slide and up to the summit, where Corona once stood. Along the summit, the side of the

Summer skiing by the summit of Rollins Pass.

road is littered with the remains of the long Corona snowshed. The west side of the summit provides a magnificent view of Winter Park ski area, the Fraser Valley, and the peaks along the Continental Divide. Several abandoned railroad trestles can be seen on the west side of the road.

The Rollins Pass area offers several interesting side roads. Travelers who wish to explore a scenic back route to the pass should begin at the Central City cemetery, a short distance west of town. From the cemetery, a good dirt road travels north to the site of Apex, which was the heart of the booming Pine Creek Mining District in the 1890s. From Apex, the route travels west through Elk Park to a ridge that gives an excellent view of the Rollins Pass area. To the left is a scenic jeeping road leading toward Kingston Peak and James Peak; to the right a road drops down the ridge to join the Rollins Pass road about five miles west of Rollinsville.

Near the top of Rollins Pass, beyond the Needle's Eye, is a Forest Service sign indicating a four-wheel-drive spur road that travels above the railroad bed along the old Boulder Pass wagon road. On the west side of the summit, below the Trestle Picnic Grounds, another side road climbs toward Rogers Pass, a high and little used pass route on the north side of James Peak.

In addition, the Rollins Pass area abounds with good hiking trails. From East Portal, a well-known hiking and cross-country skiing trail traverses the Continental Divide at Rogers Pass and descends Jim Creek to Winter Park and the West Portal of the Moffat Tunnel. From the top of Rollins Pass, another trail parallels the Continental Divide northward to Devil's Thumb Pass, which can also be reached by a road and hiking trail that extends west from the town of Eldora. Less than three miles north of Devil's Thumb Pass, also on the Continental Divide, is Arapaho Pass, a nearly 12,000-foot-high crossing that was occasionally used in the later nineteenth century to transport goods into Middle Park. At a small parking lot above Yankee Doodle Lake, a short, scenic hiking route leads to the Forest Lakes, above which are several smaller alpine lakes resting in the shadow of the Continental Divide. A short road south from the summit travels to an airplane beacon light and affords an excellent view of the area. As a result of a rock fall in the Needle's Eye tunnel, the Rollins Pass road has been closed to all through traffic for several years. Current Forest Service plans, however, call for reconstruction and reopening of the tunnel by late 1987.

5

3 Jones Pass

Location: between Berthoud Falls on US Highway 40 and Williams Fork area

Difficulty: can be traversed under good road conditions by trucks and some smaller passenger cars with adequate traction

Scenic Quality: very high with good summit view

Historic Interest: modest

Side Roads: none of special interest

High Point: 12,453 feet

Maps: USFS map of Arapaho National Forest at 1:125,000

USGS single sheet of Clear Creek County at 1:50,000

USGS sheet 4 of Grand County at 1:50,000

When the Middle Park Division of the Hayden Survey visited the area in 1873, they noted that the Jones Pass trail led down the Williams River "to within a few miles of its junction with the Grand" (Colorado). Today, the Jones Pass road begins at the site of a massive molybdenite mill and terminates less than ten miles later at a Denver Water Board closure constructed to block public access to an area where the Water Board owns a long-standing easement for the diversion of water in the Williams Fork basin. From the closure point, travelers must return along the same route used to cross Jones Pass, and no side roads of any significance diverge from the main pass road.

Despite these drawbacks, the Jones Pass road is well worth visiting for several reasons. It ranks among the most accessible backcountry pass roads over the Continental Divide. It is a relatively smooth, well-graded road due to the Denver Water Board's need for access to its collection and transmission facilities. It travels through an area of lovely forests and fine scenic views above timberline. It is lightly used even on summer weekends despite the fact that it is the highest pass in Colorado that can be reached by a

Summit view of Jones Pass.

passenger car. And the Jones Pass area is a classic case study illustrating the cumulative impact, past and present, of resource development on the high-country environment. The visual features of the area were once wholly shaped by the forces of nature; now the imprint of economic need, political demands, and technology is visible upon the land.

The Jones Pass road begins at the west end of Berthoud Falls, on US Highway 40, at the base of Berthoud Pass. Take the Henderson mine road, which is also the entrance road to the Big Bend Picnic Grounds, and at the entrance to the Henderson mine, turn right at the Jones Pass signs. The road travels up the West Fork of Clear Creek, passing several abandoned mining sites and the point where the Jones Pass Tunnel and the Vasquez Tunnel (both operated by the Denver Water Board) discharge their flow into the creek. The road continues climbing past timberline to an impressive summit perched on the Continental Divide, then descends through a zone of alpine vegetation to spruce and fir forests. Here, Englemann spruce and subalpine fir trees dominate the occasional stands of lodgepole pine and aspen. Near the road closure is the abandoned Bobtail Mine beside Bobtail Creek, a tributary of the Williams Fork River. The mine site is a scenic location nicely suited for a picnic or camping; a lengthy hiking trail leads from the site to the South Fork and Sugarloaf campgrounds, located on a spur of the Ute Pass road (*see* Ute Pass in the Summit County section).

Even though it is well graded, the Jones Pass road does present a few rough sections near the summit and should be treated with the respect due any unpaved, high-altitude pass road. Usually traffic on the road is quite light, but the Denver Water Board's heavy-construction equipment that occasionally uses the road should be treated with caution.

4 Stoney Pass

Location: between Bailey and Deckers
Difficulty: can be negotiated by most
  passenger cars under good conditions
Scenic Quality: pretty area with best views
  in the Wellington Lake area
Historic Interest: none
Side Roads: a few of interest
High Point: about 8,560 feet
Maps: USFS map of Pike National Forest
  at 1:125,000
USGS sheet 2 of Jefferson County at 1:50,000
USGS sheet 2 of Park County at 1:50,000

Afternoon shadows below Stoney Pass.

Stoney Pass, a low crossing between the North Fork of the South Platte River and its main branch, should not be confused with that high and historic route into the San Juans called Stony Pass. Little-known Stoney Pass is marked by no road signs or historical monuments, and its gentle summit rises to an elevation well below the base of many major pass routes. So why bother to include this minor crossing in a book that dwells on the high and mighty pass roads over the Colorado Rockies? The reason is simple. There are many little-traveled backcountry crossings like Stoney Pass, and exploring these lesser known routes is a rewarding experience.

Consider the case of Stoney Pass. I had decided to take a trip into the mountains in search of some bright fall colors to photograph. Once I topped Kenosha Pass and dropped down into South Park, it was clear that the aspen had lost their glow: barren trunks banded the hillsides. To make matters worse, the road to Georgia Pass (*see* section on Summit County passes) was heavy with truck traffic, and the roar of chainsaws blasted from the woods. On this, the last weekend before the start of the deer hunting season, weekend lumberjacks were stockpiling pine in anticipation of another cold winter.

I did not linger on Georgia Pass, and the afternoon was still young as I descended from Kenosha Pass into the South Platte Valley. Rather than return home directly, I decided to explore a route that I had noticed earlier on a Forest Service map. Turning southeast at Bailey, I dipped down into Pike National Forest toward Wellington Lake and Stoney Pass. One-half dozen miles from Bailey and the bustle of traffic on US Highway 285, the road turned into a quiet, winding lane reminiscent of the back roads and lake-studded rolling hills that I used to travel in New England and southern Ontario. Here, at a lower elevation, the aspen were at the height of their

glory, reflecting a golden glow of yellow and crisp orange in the late afternoon sunshine. Here, too, were the scenes for which I had been looking: the brightly colored leaves framing a view of Wellington Lake and above it the nicely sculptured rock form identified on my map as The Castle. Beyond the top of Stoney Pass, the bands of colorful aspen disappeared, but the route down Cabin Creek to the South Platte was a lovely journey through forests of mature pine undisturbed by the shriek of chainsaws or the choking dust of heavily laden trucks.

To reach Stoney Pass from the north, take US Highway 285 to the east end of Bailey, and turn south at the edge of town. Five miles from the turnoff, take the right-hand fork marked as the route to Wellington Lake. The route then leads directly over the summit. At the south end of the Stoney Pass road, a traveler can choose from among a variety of exit routes. In one direction is Chessman Lake and a long, winding back road to Tarryall Reservoir or, by another route, US Highway 24. Alternately, a paved county road returns north to US Highway 285 at Pine Junction, and another county road leads along the South Platte River and over the edge of the Rampart Range to US Highway 85 at Sedalia. As a further temptation to the back road explorer, additional side roads branch off from every one of these exit routes.

8

The Castle rising above Wellington Lake.

5 Guanella Pass

Location: between Georgetown on Interstate 70 and Grant on US Highway 285
Difficulty: can be negotiated by all passenger cars under good conditions
Scenic Quality: very attractive summit area with excellent mountain views
Historic Interest: slight
Side Roads: several of interest
High Point: 11,669 feet
Maps: USFS map of Arapaho National Forest at 1:125,000
USGS single sheet of Clear Creek County at 1:50,000
USGS sheet 2 of Park County at 1:50,000
Colorado highway map at 1:1,000,000

The Guanella Pass road provides a convenient and easily negotiated back route link, a portion of which is paved, between Georgetown and US Highway 285. Because the Guanella Pass road is both scenic and readily accessible, the area is intensively used on a year-round basis for a variety of recreational purposes that include camping, hiking, hunting, cross-country, and alpine skiing (at the Geneva Basin ski area). A half dozen Forest Service campgrounds and picnic grounds dot the twenty-four-mile route from Georgetown to Grant, and numerous hiking/skiing trails take off from the southern portion of the road. The pass route honors Byron Guanella, a former county road supervisor and descendant of an early Georgetown family.

From Georgetown, the Guanella Pass road

The Sawtooth and Mt. Bierstadt from the Guanella Pass summit.

ascends Leavenworth Mountain and climbs up South Clear Creek, passing a hydroelectric generating plant and the turnoff for Argentine Pass (*see* section on Summit County passes). As the summit approaches, Mt. Bierstadt and the Sawtooth, readily identified by its name, dominate the scenery to the east. From the alpine summit of Guanella Pass, located just above timberline, the Sawtooth, Mt. Bierstadt, and behind it Mt. Evans rise to the east. To the west is an unobstructed view of the Continental Divide in the area between Webster Pass and Argentine Pass. Descending from the summit, the road skirts Duck Lake, an alpine lake above the Geneva Basin ski area, and drops into a wide, scenic meadow. A series of trails paralleling the major drainages in the area give access to the backcountry, and a side road at the Duck Creek Picnic Grounds ascends Geneva Creek, ending above

timberline by several abandoned mines about 1,000 feet below the Continental Divide. This side road, which deteriorates to a jeep trail, provides the only motorized access to the eastern side of the Continental Divide in the area between Webster Pass and Argentine Pass. Less than a mile from the end of the road lies the Peru Mining District and a road into the town of Montezuma. The town is less than three miles distant as the crow flies, but the Divide blocks the way to all but the most intrepid climbers.

Route finding in the Guanella Pass area is a refreshingly simple matter. Both from Grant and Georgetown, the Guanella Pass road is well marked. At Grant, simply turn north. In Georgetown, proceed one mile from the I-70 exit to the west end of the town, where the road begins to climb Leavenworth Mountain.

The Sawtooth and Mt. Bierstadt looming above the Guanella Pass Road.

6 Mosquito Pass

Location: between Fairplay and Leadville
Difficulty: four-wheel-drive required
Scenic Quality: very high, with spectacular alpine views
Historic Interest: very high
Side Roads: many of historic and scenic value
High Point: 13,188 feet
Maps: USFS map of San Isabel National Forest at 1:125,000
USFS map of Pike National Forest at 1:125,000
USGS sheet 1 of Park County at 1:50,000
USGS single sheet of Lake County at 1:50,000
Colorado highway map at 1:1,000,000

The Mosquito Pass road, like the roads over Argentine Pass on the Continental Divide and Pearl Pass over the Elk Range, was a road too high. In each case, these highest pass roads in the Rockies were daring and short-lived attempts to develop *the* most direct route to the pot of gold or silver at the end of the rainbow. All three pass roads failed within a few years, to be replaced by less direct but surer routes. Of these three pass roads, Mosquito Pass has remained the best known. The reasons are several. The Mosquito Pass road is simply the highest such road still open in Colorado, the nation, or the Rocky Mountains (Argentine Pass is a bit higher but is closed on the west side). The pass road has been used for a generation to hold the annual Leadville to Fairplay World's Championship Mosquito Pass Burro Race. And finally, the Mosquito Pass toll road served the Leadville area—a mining district so vast in its wealth, so long-lived, and so excessive in its habits that nearly everything associated with it has become legend.

Mosquito Pass began as a precariously high trail over the Mosquito Range and was used occasionally to reach placer gold discovered in the early 1860s near present-day Leadville. F. V. Hayden's 1877 *Atlas of Colorado* shows only a trail stretching from Alma, near Fairplay, over Mosquito Pass to the early mining town of Oro City, located in California Gulch. In 1873, a Hayden Survey party placed the pass elevation at 13,438 feet, noting that the ascent was steep and difficult on both sides for pack animals. During 1878, vast deposits of silver were discovered in California Gulch, and a stampede of unprecedented proportions began. As waves of fortune seekers descended on the area, its population quickly swelled from several hundred to ten thousand. In those incredible days when nothing seemed impossible, local interests formed the Mosquito Pass Wagon Road Company to blast a road where Father Dyer, the itinerant preacher and carrier of the mails, had traveled on his Norwegian skis more than a decade earlier.

In less than a year of frenzied activity, the road was completed, and by the summer of 1879 some 150 wagons, freighters, and stagecoaches were traveling over Mosquito Pass daily. Unfortunately for the Leadville and Fairplay investors in the Mosquito Pass Wagon Road Company, while their work crews were toiling up the mountain, railroadmen from both the Denver and South Park and the Denver and Rio Grande (now the Denver and Rio Grande Western) railroads were just as quickly laying down track in the direction of Leadville. By the summer of 1880, both

Mosquito Gulch in early winter

lines had reached Leadville, and little reason remained to struggle over the steep pitches and rough surface of the Mosquito Pass toll road. The road was soon abandoned, and so it remained until after the conclusion of World War II, when local residents restored the route to a semblance of its former self for the first of the annual Mosquito Pass burro races.

The yearly burro races are now a well-established rite in the Leadville-Fairplay area, and the pass road is generally open for motorized travel from mid-July to early September. Stories abound of passenger cars that successfully complete the trip, but the Mosquito Pass road is neither a safe nor enjoyable route for such vehicles—even when approached from the more readily negotiable east side. Having once traveled by motorcycle from Leadville over the summit and back down the west side when the roadway was covered with fresh snow, slush, and mud, I also do not recommend trying the Mosquito Pass road under inclement weather conditions. The fair weather scenery is simply too good and the trip too enjoyable to be marred by unfavorable circumstances.

The road to Mosquito Pass from the east starts on Colorado Highway 9 about six miles north of Fairplay at the junction with the Mosquito Gulch road. A high-quality gravel road travels through the historic Mosquito Creek mining area and forks left along South Mosquito Creek, traveling south of London Mountain. The nineteenth-century toll road route led up the main branch of Mosquito Creek along a more gentle grade on the north side of London Mountain. The road then climbs steeply to American Flats, and at the end of this imposing alpine meadow it becomes a shelf route to the pass summit, where a glorious view unfolds. To the east is the broad expanse of South Park; to the west lies Leadville and the upper Arkansas Valley, Turquoise Reservoir, and more than one dozen of the 14,000-foot peaks that cap the Sawatch Range. About sixteen miles directly west is Hagerman Pass and below it the Roaring Fork Valley. At the pass summit is a small stone memorial to Father Dyer, the "Snowshoe Itinerant." The west side descent begins steeply then levels out at Evans Gulch, where a graveled road travels past the famous Matchless mine (which earned Leadville's silver king, H. A. W. Tabor, $10 million). In Leadville it becomes 7th Street East, and it joins US Highway 24 in downtown Leadville.

Both the Fairplay and Leadville sides of Mosquito Pass are honeycombed with a network of roads leading up the various drainages to mine sites, mills, and long-abandoned cabins. At the top of Mosquito Pass, a side road ascends north to the summit of Mosquito Peak, affording an excellent view of the massive formation that includes Mt. Democrat, Mt. Cameron, Mt. Lincoln, and Mt. Bross (all fourteeners). To the west of the summit area, another side road travels a short distance south to the ridge of the Mosquito Range and terminates at a meteorological transmitting station.

Turquoise Reservoir and the Sawatch Range from the Mosquito Pass road.

7 Weston Pass

Location: between South Park on US Highway 285 and the upper Arkansas River valley on US Highway 24
Difficulty: can be negotiated by most passenger cars under good conditions
Scenic Quality: pretty area with especially attractive views on east side
Historic Interest: high
Side Roads: several of considerable interest
High Point: 11,921 feet
Maps: USFS map of Pike National Forest at 1:125,000
USFS map of San Isabel National Forest at 1:125,000
USGS sheet 3 of Park County at 1:50,000
USGS single sheet of Lake County at 1:50,000
Colorado highway map at 1:1,000,000

For many years, Weston Pass was a common route from the broad expanse of South Park into the Leadville area. Originally an Indian trail, the Weston Pass route became a wagon road during the California Gulch mining boom of 1860. Dur-

ing the early days of that first Leadville boom, the pass road was clogged with traffic and thick with dust as a steady stream of wagons traveled back and forth between Weston and the mining camps around Leadville. The town of Weston, which died with the coming of the railroad, served as the eastern terminus of the pass road. At its peak, the town included nearly a dozen restaurants along with a substantial number of bars, gambling parlors, and warehouses.

The Wall and Witter Stage Company provided freight and passenger service over the pass. At its peak, the company boasted an inventory of 400 horses, 7 stagecoaches, and 11 express wagons. Business was sufficiently brisk that in 1879 the company collected nearly $1.5 million in fares as travelers streamed into the Leadville area. That same year saw the completion of the Mosquito Pass road, and a year later both General Palmer's narrow gauge railroad and the Denver, South Park, and Pacific line had reached Leadville, thereby dooming both Weston and the Wall and Witter Stage Company.

Hayden's 1877 *Atlas of Colorado* shows the Mosquito Pass route as no more than a trail con-

East side view of the Weston Pass road.

necting Alma, on the western edge of South Park, with California Gulch and the mining town of Oro City. The Weston Pass route then provided the only direct road into the upper portion of the Arkansas Valley. The Hayden Survey explored Weston Pass in 1873, finding there a good wagon road with an easy ascent on the east side and steeper grades on the Arkansas Valley side. The importance of Weston Pass resulted from the geography of the area. The Weston Pass road, though higher than Berthoud Pass, is more than 1,000 feet below Mosquito Pass and still provides a reasonably direct route from Fairplay to Leadville. The Mosquito Pass road was—and is today—a steep, rough route over a long stretch of exposed terrain, while the Weston Pass area allows a more gentle and less demanding route over the southern end of the Mosquito Range. An even lower road crossed into the Arkansas Valley at Trout Creek Pass (9,346 feet), the route used by Captain Zebulon Pike and later, in the 1880s, by the Denver, South Park, and Pacific railroad. But this route more than doubled the distance from Fairplay to Leadville via Weston Pass.

The modern Weston Pass road is a well-marked and relatively smooth route that the majority of passenger cars can travel once the snow has melted and the roadway has dried. Starting at US Highway 285 south of Fairplay, a maintained gravel road travels across broad meadows of lush grass and through a zone of aspen to the point where the road parallels the South Fork of the South Platte River. From there, the road climbs smoothly up to the headwaters of the South Fork and crosses the summit of Weston Pass well above timberline. The west side offers an attractive valley and excellent views of the Collegiate Range.

The Weston Pass area also offers a variety of interesting side roads. About a mile north of the Weston Pass road cutoff, another road runs west from US Highway 285. About three miles from the highway the road forks; to the right is the route to Brown's Pass (about 11,000 feet), and to the left is the route to Breakneck Pass (about 10,900 feet). It matters little which way a traveler turns since the two passes are connected by a loop road extending along Sheep Creek. In addition, a high-quality Forest Service road starting on US Highway 285 about a mile south of Fairplay travels to Fourmile Campground and, above that, to several abandoned mining sites near the crest of the Mosquito Range at a point where the high peaks approach—and in the case of Mt. Sherman—exceed 14,000 feet in elevation. In addition, a short road travels from the top of Weston Pass to the summit of a hill just south of the pass, affording a better view of the surrounding countryside.

Route finding in the Weston Pass area presents no difficulties. The east side of the pass road is located about five miles south of Fairplay on US Highway 285 and is indicated by a large sign; another Forest Service access road about six miles farther south on US Highway 285 also leads into the pass road. On the west side, Weston Pass is reached from a well-marked side road that begins on US Highway 24 about six miles south of Leadville.

Wet Mountain Valley view of the Sangre de Cristos.

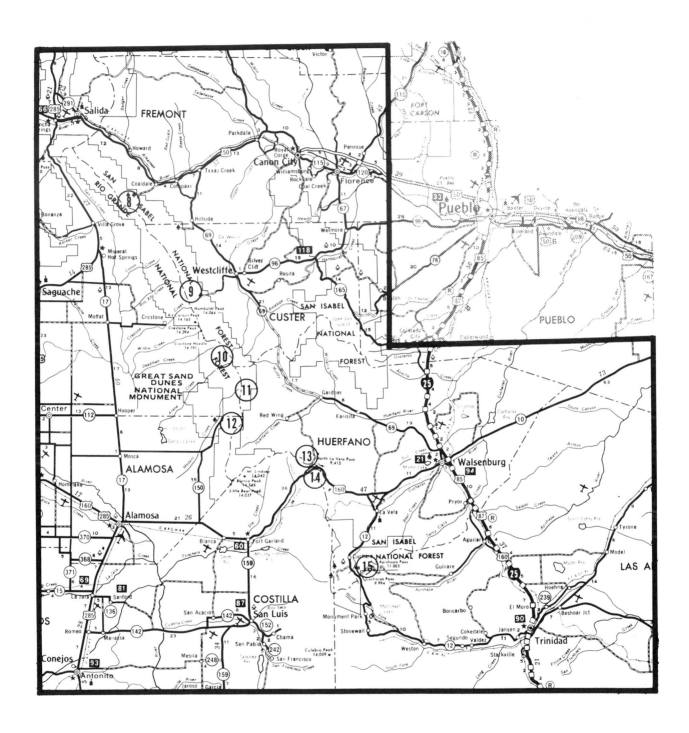

Part Two
Sangre de Cristo Passes

Since time immemorial, the Sangre de Cristo Mountains have been a barrier: a retaining wall that blocked the millions of tons of sand blowing across the San Luis Valley eons ago, a barrier that protected settlers from attack, an impediment to commerce and trade first among the Spanish, then among the English and other European settlers. A century before the pilgrims landed at Plymouth Rock, Spanish explorers began to probe northward from Mexico into the lower arm of the Sangre de Cristos. Where the Utes, Apache raiding parties, and Pueblo Indians had traveled for centuries, the Spanish looked but did not conquer. Spanish governors saw the Sangre de Cristos as the far boundary of their political influence. Spanish explorers and churchmen reared in an age of intense religious fervor saw in that same range images of their faith writ large. Sangre de Cristo means "Blood of Christ" in Spanish—an appropriate name for a mountain range that reflects such unearthly colors from the setting sun.

As the Spanish dreams of empire in the New World faded, a new Anglo-American culture pushed westward. First came traders and trappers followed by Army explorers, surveyors, railroad men, and settlers. In the early 1870s, the Southern Division of the famous Hayden Survey hauled their barometers, transits, and other scientific instruments into the Sangre de Cristos. They left not only with a wealth of geographic, geological, and botanical information, but they also took home a strong sense of setting. In the ninth *Annual Report of the United States Geological and Geographical Survey*, published in 1877, a member of the expedition wrote of the Sangre de Cristo Range:

> Its highest peaks, presenting the boldest outlines, look very forbidding when seen standing in relief against the sky. The evenness of the most elevated points, the symmetry of form, and the fields of snow that never disappear entirely lend this range a charm that can never be forgotten by one who has seen it.

The young energetic scientists of the Hayden Survey, educated at eastern universities, were dispassionate students of topography, geology, botany, natural history, and ethnology. What they found in the Rockies not only filled their notebooks with many thousand pages of data but also filled their minds with a sense of awe and wonderment.

Because they contain few commercially valuable mineral deposits and because the main routes of civilization lie elsewhere, the Sangre de Cristos are little changed from the days of the Spanish Empire. There is a relative absence of the mining pits, tailings ponds, ski trails, and asphalt highways so evident elsewhere in the Colorado Rockies. Especially in the high Sangre de Cristos, where the crest of the range runs in an almost unbroken line at the 13,000-foot level, man's imprint on the workings of nature is scarcely visible.

Nevertheless, the impact of civilization on the Sangre de Cristo Range exists in the series of crossings that traverse the range: Hayden Pass south of Salida, Hermit Pass, Music Pass, Medano Pass, Mosca Pass, the La Veta passes, and several lesser routes, all of which were developed at different times and for different purposes. Toll roads were constructed where trails once led, and the toll roads were in turn abandoned in favor of the path that steam-driven locomotives followed. In the case of La Veta Pass, when the steel rails were relocated elsewhere a modern highway appeared, then switched its course, leaving still another crumbling memorial to earlier times.

The science of geology teaches that the multilayer levels of soil, rock, and minerals chronicle the physical history of our planet. Once we learn how to read that silent chronicle, the geological past and present become clearer. So, too, do the ebb and flow of transportation routes chronicle the political and economic history of the peoples who have inhabited an area. The Sangre de Cristo pass routes are a multilayered chronicle of the cultural and technological changes that swept through the southern valleys of Colorado in the past three centuries.

8 Hayden Pass

Location: between Coaldale in the
    Arkansas Valley and Villa Grove
    in the San Luis Valley
Difficulty: four-wheel-drive recommended on
    both sides of the pass
Scenic Quality: best views on lower portion
    of west side
Historic Interest: moderate
Side Roads: few in the area
High Point: 10,709 feet
Maps: USFS map of San Isabel National
    Forest at 1:125,000 or
USFS map of Rio Grande National Forest
    at 1:125,000
USGS sheet 1 of Fremont County at 1:50,000
USGS sheet 2 of Saguache County at 1:50,000

Hayden Pass, the most northerly road through the Sangre de Cristos, is little known and infrequently used today. But in the 1880s, this conveniently located crossing from the Arkansas River to the upper San Luis Valley was a popular route westward to the mining camps around Bonanza and to the Cochetopa Pass road (*see* Gunnison County section) into Gunnison country. Even before the silver strikes near Bonanza, the route was widely used; it is shown by name and depicted as a trail in Hayden's 1877 *Atlas of Colorado.*

For travelers westward bound on the Arkansas River to the San Luis Valley, the Hayden Pass crossing eliminated the need to continue upstream to Salida, go west to Poncha Springs, and take the Poncha Pass route into the head of the valley. The Hayden Pass summit is less than ten miles from the waters of the Arkansas River, and after a short, steep descent, the west side of the route travels directly down the gentle western flank of the range to Villa Grove. From Villa Grove, once an important supply center, a seventeen-mile toll road built by Otto Mears went westward across the valley and up Kerber Creek to Bonanza.

The present east side route to Hayden Pass,

The San Luis Valley from the Hayden Pass road.

named not for the famous surveyor but in honor of a local rancher, starts on US Highway 50 four miles west of Cotopaxi and twenty-one miles south of Salida at a sign indicating the route to Hayden Campground. About a mile beyond the campground, take an unmarked side road to the left, which climbs steeply in places through thick pine forests to an unspectacular summit. The west side of the road proceeds down several steep pitches before emerging dramatically from tree line at a point where a sweeping view unfolds. Stretched out below is the floor of the San Luis Valley, rimmed on the west by the low line of the San Juans and protected on the east by the curved flanks of the Sangre de Cristos. From this vantage point, the Hayden Pass road can be seen sweeping gently down to Villa Grove, and the road west to Kerber Creek and Bonanza is clearly visible on the valley floor. The remainder of the trip to Villa Grove is anticlimactic, a smooth and relaxed journey with attractive valley views of the Sangre de Cristos rising in a long, unbroken line.

On the east side of Hayden Pass are few side roads of interest, but the Rainbow Trail bisects the pass route a short distance beyond the turnoff to Hayden Pass. The Rainbow Trail, a fifty-five-mile-long route built in the World War II era for fire control, is open to hikers, horseback travel, and motorcycles.

On the west side of the pass, about two and one-half miles beyond Villa Grove, side roads branch to the north and the south. The road to the north travels a roundabout route along the edge of the Sangre de Cristos, and additional side roads branch out along the drainages. The road to the south leads also along the edge of the range to Valley View Hot Springs, an old resort spa. From Valley View Hot Springs, a road continues south, giving access to several Forest Service routes into the Sangre de Cristos. These west side roads are particularly attractive to travel in the late afternoon, when the low sun angle and dramatic cloud formations contribute an added dimension to the area.

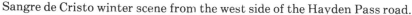

Sangre de Cristo winter scene from the west side of the Hayden Pass road.

9 Hermit Pass

Location: between Westcliffe and the San
 Luis Valley
Difficulty: four-wheel-drive required to reach
 the summit
Scenic Quality: imposing area with dramatic
 alpine scenery
Historic Interest: slight
Side Roads: few available
High Point: about 13,020 feet
Maps: USFS map of San Isabel National Forest
 at 1:125,000
USFS map of Rio Grande National Forest
 at 1:125,000
USGS sheet 1 of Custer County at 1:50,000
USGS sheet 5 of Saguache County at 1:50,000

No wagon road or railroad tracks ever
climbed over Hermit Pass, and few if any persons
of rank or distinction are reported to have
traveled the Hermit Pass road. But what Hermit
Pass lacks in historical interest or fame it more
than compensates for with its impressive
scenery. Several other pass trails over the Sangre
de Cristos reach approximately the same elevation, but no other pass road in this range ascends
nearly so high. In fact, the Hermit Pass summit,
which is a bit more than 13,000 feet, ranks with
Mosquito Pass, Argentine Pass, and Imogene
Pass as among the highest pass routes in the nation that can be reached by motor vehicle (conditions permitting, of course).

The route to Hermit Pass, which is accessible
to vehicles only from the east, begins on the south
side of Westcliffe at Colorado Highway 69. Take
the Hermit Lake road west about seven miles to
the National Forest boundary. The road ascends
along the rushing waters of the Middle Fork of
Taylor Creek and climbs through a lovely pine
forest that occasionally opens onto meadows that
offer a view of the high peaks that lie just south
of Hermit Pass. As the road rises past timberline,
a magnificent alpine expanse unfolds beneath the

The Hermit Pass road emerging from timberline.

13,000-foot crest line of the Sangre de Cristos. Ahead are the flanks of Hermit Peak and Eureka Mountain; to the right, the angular ridge of Rio Alto Peak reaches to nearly 14,000 feet. Along the route to the summit is Hermit Lake and then Horseshoe Lake, situated well above timberline. Hermit Peak and Eureka Mountain stand on the south side of the pass summit; on the north is 13,794-foot-high Rito Alto Peak. The Hayden Survey lists Rito Alto as one of the primary points of triangulation used more than a century ago to map the Colorado mountains. But it is unlikely that the survey crews ever climbed Rito Alto; the peak by that name in the 1877 and 1881 Hayden atlases of Colorado is now called Cottonwood Peak, located about nine miles farther north along the Sangre de Cristo Range.

From the top of Hermit Pass a magnificent view appears. To the east is the Wet Mountain Valley and beyond it, the Great Plains. To the west lies the San Luis Valley, rimmed on the far side by the San Juan Mountains. South of the pass rises the Crestone Group and Kit Carson (all of these are fourteeners). The drainages that descend down the west side of the Sangre de Cristos promise the start of a significant river. But this promise never materializes. The creeks terminate in the northern portion of the valley, which is a closed basin from which no surface water escapes. Beneath the porous valley floor, however, lies an untapped reservoir of groundwater, or aquifer, which is one of the largest such water bodies in the world.

Few side roads of interest exist in the Hermit Pass area, but hiking trails are available in abundance. From the west side, Hermit Pass can be reached by long but scenic trails that ascend Rito Alto Creek or Cotton Creek. About three miles south of the Hermit Pass road, at the Alvarado Campground, and Abbots Lodge, by the National Forest boundary, is the start of a long loop trail over Comanche Pass and Venable Pass. An alternate route through Phantom Terrace connects the two pass routes. The Venable trail descends beside the Venable Lakes and Venable Falls to Abbots Lodge and the Alvarado Campground. Backcountry hikers intending to travel these high routes should consult Robert Ormes' *Guide to the Colorado Mountains* or a similar source of route-finding information.

A mountainscape view from the Hermitt Pass road.

10 Music Pass

Location: between the Wet Mountain Valley and the San Luis Valley

Difficulty: four-wheel-drive strongly recommended

Scenic Quality: very attractive area

Historic Interest: modest

Side Roads: a few of high scenic value

High Point: about 11,380 feet

Maps: USFS map of San Isabel National Forest at 1:125,000

USFS map of Rio Grande National Forest at 1:125,000

USGS sheet 1 of Custer County at 1:50,000

USGS sheet 5 of Saguache County at 1:50,000

Music Pass, located north of Medano and Mosca passes, crosses the Sangre de Cristo Range at a point substantially higher than these neighboring routes; hence, it was little used historically as a passageway to the San Luis Valley.

Hayden's survey crews knew of Music Pass, though they confused it with Medano Pass, and the route was probably traveled by mountain men, Spanish traders, and the far-ranging Ute Indians. But the absence of commercially valuable mineral deposits in the area and the availability of lower routes provided little reason to use Music Pass.

According to the conventional explanation, Music Pass acquired its name from the musical tone of the winds blowing through the area. Some sources say it is the sound of the wind whistling along the sand dunes, which are about eight miles southwest of the summit; other persons attribute the sound to the wind howling among rocks or mountain ridges in the area. Drainage ways can sometimes act as an acoustical funnel, and ridge walls work like a sounding board, transmitting or even amplifying sounds. Visitors to the area are welcome to seek their own explanation, but recent scientific evidence suggests that the elusive strains of music, if they exist at all, probably

Sangre de Cristo view of the route to Music Pass.

arise from shearing forces that accumulate in the loosely settled sand, producing horizontal avalanches that generate a distinctive sound. The phenomenon of "singing sands" is known to occur at several dozen sites around the world.

The route to Music Pass begins on the east side of the Sangre de Cristos. From Westcliffe, travel four and one-half miles south on Colorado Highway 69 and turn south on the Colfax Lane road. This well-paved road, which gives a picture-book view of Humboldt Peak and other 14,000-foot peaks behind it, forks after about five miles. The Music Pass road goes east (left) around a curve, then begins climbing gently to the National Forest boundary. The road ascends through a lovely pine forest, but the occasionally rough surface and steep berms across the roadway are an impediment to most two-wheel-drive vehicles. Near the summit, several short side roads diverge to the left, while the main route travels to the right, dropping steeply to a meadow and then climbing again into a heavily timbered area. The road ends at a Forest Service parking area about one mile from the summit; the trail to the top of Music Pass can be reached either on foot or by motorcycle. On the west side of the summit, in Rio Grande National Forest, motorized travel is prohibited.

Music Pass can also be reached from the west side of the Sangre de Cristos, but the several routes available require a lengthy hike. The most common route starts in the area of Hooper on Colorado Highway 17 and crosses the old Luis Maria Baca Grant. From the abandoned town site of Liberty, a trail extends about a dozen miles up Sand Creek and joins the Music Pass trail about a mile northwest of the pass summit. Since permission to cross this portion of the Baca Grant has been difficult to obtain, Great Sand Dunes National Monument staff suggest two alternate routes: either hike northeast cross-country from the Medano Creek jeep road and intersect the Sand Creek trail, or go east from Moffat on Colorado Highway 17 to the town of Crestone and, after obtaining permission to cross private land, travel southeast through the Baca Grant by way of a jeep road to the townsite of Duncan, and from there travel on foot or horseback up the Sand Creek trail to the Music Pass cutoff. The Luis Maria Baca Grant is crisscrossed by a complex network of roads, however, so travelers through this area should ask locally for guidance and take the appropriate maps.

Several interesting side trips are available in the Music Pass area. Foremost among them is the four-wheel-drive road up Colony Creek to the South Colony Lakes, Crestone Peak and Crestone Needle. The lakes are are a short hike from the road and afford an excellent view of the Crestones, which are two of the most difficult fourteeners in Colorado to climb. The roads to Hermit Pass and Medano Pass are within a dozen miles of the Music Pass road, and the famous Rainbow Trail starts its long traverse of the Sangre de Cristos at the Music Pass road.

11 Medano Pass

Location: between the Wet Mountain Valley
   and Great Sand Dunes National Monument
Difficulty: requires four-wheel-drive
Scenic Quality: excellent scenery and striking
   sights on west side
Historic Interest: considerable
Side Roads: few of interest
High Point: about 9,950 feet
Maps: USFS map of San Isabel National
   Forest at 1:125,000
USFS map of Rio Grande National Forest
   at 1:125,000
USGS sheet 1 of Huerfano County at 1:50,000
USGS sheet 5 of Saguache County at 1:50,000

This pass route from the Wet Mountain
Valley across the Sangre de Cristo Mountains to
the San Luis Valley was established by nomadic
Indians long before Captain Zebulon Pike led his
expedition on a winter crossing in 1807. Pike had
started out the previous summer to search for the
headwaters of the Arkansas River and from there
to travel south by way of the Red River. Earlier in
his journey, Pike tried but failed to climb the mountain that bears his name. Less certain is the location
where his expedition crossed the Sangre de Cristos.
It probably was at the place called Pike's Gap. But
the name did not stick. The older and more appropriate Spanish name, Medano ("sand hill"), has
persisted. The pass was crossed again in 1853 by
Captain John Gunnison, who was leading a government expedition from Kansas City to California in
search of railroad routes through the Rockies.

Upon descending from Medano Pass, the
Pike and Gunnison expeditions came upon a phenomenon that still amazes modern travelers: massive barren dunes of sand resting at the edge of a
huge valley. Medano Pass is a low gateway,
framed at each end by a cluster of 14,000-foot
mountains, leading to this striking accident of
geology. Not even Mosca Pass, which is a few
miles to the south, offers an entrance to the sand

Medano Pass route with the sand dunes and the Sangre de Cristos in the background.

dunes that can rival Medano Pass for its drama and the abrupt change in landscape it offers.

The Medano Pass road begins on the east in the scenic Wet Mountain Valley on State Highway 69, about twenty-four miles south of Westcliffe and eight miles north of Gardner. The pass route is marked by a "Medano Road" Forest Service sign and a Huerfano County 17 sign. From this intersection, the road slowly climbs along privately owned grazing lands and then ascends more steeply through pine and aspen to a wooded summit that is hardly noticeable. West of the summit, the road drops steeply along a series of narrow steps, which must be negotiated with caution, then traverses a lovely valley rich with vegetation and protected to the north by a high rock wall. The sandy soils in the valley are mute evidence of the wind that ages ago drifted this finely ground debris up the mountain gap and are also a harbinger of the vast sand dunes that lie ahead.

A short distance beyond the valley, a gate and sign mark the eastern boundary of the Great Sand Dunes National Monument. At this point, motorized travelers should stop to reduce the air pressure in their vehicle tires and, depending on conditions, apply a thick coating of insect repellent to ward off the rapacious mosquito swarms that periodically infest the area. Beyond the park boundary lies an open, sandy grassland that dramatically signals the shift from mountain to desert terrain, and beyond this transitional zone the route drops into Medano Creek, which Captain Pike may have mistaken briefly for the Red River and which the Hayden Survey nearly fifty years later labeled as Sand Creek. Modern visitors will discover, as Pike did, that Medano Creek, which is rarely more than ankle-deep in the Monument, soon disappears beneath the creek bed, and the route continues along a treacherously soft sand wash. Here, on a Sunday afternoon in the summer, I have seen the spectacle of massive four-wheel-drive vehicles, wheels spinning and immobilized in the sand, looking like the mechanized desert counterpart of those ancient swamp creatures fatally trapped in the bottomless mire of a distant geologic era.

Before venturing across this dry land, the wise traveler will spend a while by the cool waters of Medano Creek, relaxing in the shadow of the sand dunes. Beyond the sand wash lies Piñon Flats Campground and an asphalt highway leading back to civilization. About a mile south of the campground is the visitor center, where a fascinating and detailed Park Service presentation on the natural history of the area can be enjoyed in air-conditioned comfort. Just north of the center, at a parking lot, begins the trail eastward to Mosca Pass, the summit of which is about three miles distant. A bit south of the visitor center is a service road, where compressed air is available for reinflating tires.

The access road to Great Sand Dunes National Monument and Medano Pass leads west to State Highway 17 and south to US 160. From out on the wide valley floor, a sweeping panorama comes into view: the sand dunes framed from behind by the Sangre de Cristo Range, which rises on the south to a trio of 14,000-foot peaks (Blanca, Lindsey, and Little Bear) and on the north to a quartet of fourteeners (Kit Carson, Humboldt, Crestone Needle, and Crestone Peak).

12 Mosca Pass

Location: between Gardner in the Wet
   Mountain Valley and Great Sand Dunes
   National Monument
Difficulty: most of the east side route
   passable by smaller passenger cars
Scenic Quality: very attractive area with
   lovely valleys
Historic Interest: high
Side Roads: many of interest in the area
High Point: 9,713 feet
Maps: USFS map of San Isabel National
   Forest at 1:125,000
USFS map of Rio Grande National Forest
   at 1:125,000
USGS sheet 1 of Huerfano County at 1:50,000
USGS sheet 1 of Alamosa County at 1:50,000

Like Medano Pass, the Mosca (Spanish for "fly") Pass route traverses the Sangre de Cristos from the Wet Mountain Valley to the San Luis Valley. But Mosca Pass, about eight miles south of Medano Pass, is a bit lower than its northern neighbor and served more frequently as a route westward.

The history of Mosca Pass as a gateway for exploration and commerce by European settlers reaches back to the eighteenth century. In the 1820s, Antoine Robidoux, an American trader and explorer of French-Canadian descent, traveled the Mosca Pass route, called for a time Robidoux Pass, with pack trains destined for the Gunnison country and the Green River area in Utah. Captain Gunnison's ill-fated expedition of 1853 in search of railroad routes to California ex-

The west side of Mosca Pass.

plored the Mosca Pass trail, finding it a better pass route than Medano Pass but wholly unsuitable for a rail line over the Sangre de Cristos. In the early 1870s, one of Hayden's field survey teams explored the Mosca Pass area, finding there a wagon toll road in use. The San Juan mining boom, then in its early stages, received a portion of its supplies from Pueblo by way of the route over Mosca Pass and across the San Luis Valley.

By 1877, General William Jackson Palmer had pushed his Denver and Rio Grande Railway tracks over La Veta Pass and on to Alamosa. Five years later, D&RG track extended all the way to Durango and Silverton by way of Cumbres Pass and a variety of other high-mountain gateways. The arrival of narrow gauge, steam-driven travel hastened the doom of many mountain toll roads, including the Mosca Pass road, which lost out to the longer but more gentle La Veta route.

Today, in fact, the Mosca Pass route is blocked by the Forest Service to motorized travel a short distance west of the summit. From the point of closure, a three-and-one-half-mile hiking and horseback trail extends down Mosca Creek, ending at the asphalt highway in Great Sand Dunes National Monument. Nevertheless, a trip over Mosca Pass, with or without the hike down to the sand dunes, ranks among the most enjoyable pass road trips in the Sangre de Cristo Range. Though less spectacular than the rugged, alpine terrain of Hermit Pass, the Mosca Pass route offers a succession of lovely and unspoiled countryside.

From Gardner on Colorado Highway 69, the Mosca Pass road travels southwest through the stunning Huerfano River valley beside lush irrigated meadows and old stands of cottonwood. About eleven miles from Gardner, the route bends to the right along the narrow confines of May Creek and then opens up through a wide, shallow meadow that yields an excellent view of Mt. Lindsey and Blanca Peak. At the summit of Mosca Pass, the road surface becomes a bit rough and then ends for motorized travel in a secluded meadow a short distance beyond the top of the pass. From this excellent picnicking site, it is only a moderate hike down to the sand dunes and back up Mosca Creek.

Almost the entire length of the route from Gardner up May Creek is studded with side roads wandering off in nearly every direction, and by continuing along the Huerfano Valley road beyond the Mosca Pass cutoff, a traveler can ascend through unspoiled countryside toward the flanks of Blanca Peak and Little Bear. Most of these roads are in good condition, since they are used regularly by local ranchers. But nearly all the valley is privately owned or leased, so inquiries should be made to avoid trespassing.

Route finding in the Mosca Pass area presents few difficulties. Just north of Gardner on Colorado Highway 69, the Huerfano Valley road branches to the west. Follow this road through Red Wing to the Mosca Pass turnoff at May Creek, marked by a sign indicating that the summit of Mosca Pass is seven miles ahead. Beyond this point, several side roads head to the north. Bear to the left and stay on the route to Mosca Pass. Many hiking trails are located throughout the upper tributaries of the Huerfano River and are described by Robert Ormes in his *Guide to the Colorado Mountains.*

13 Pass Creek Pass

Location: between Gardner in the Wet
Mountain Valley and US Highway 160 west
of North La Veta Pass
Difficulty: can be negotiated by most
passenger cars under normal conditions
Scenic Quality: pretty countryside with
summit view of the Spanish Peaks
Historic Interest: substantial
Side Roads: several available in the area
High Point: about 9,400 feet
Maps: USFS map of San Isabel National
Forest at 1:125,000
USGS sheet 1 of Huerfano County at 1:50,000
USGS sheet 1 of Costilla County at 1:50,000

In 1779, while the American colonies were
battling for their independence from England,
Juan Bautista de Anza, then governor of New
Mexico, led an expedition from Santa Fe to sub-
due the Comanches and to explore the hinterland
surrounding the Spanish Empire in the New
World. After massacring a suitable number of
Comanche men, women, and children, de Anza returned home across the Sangre de Cristos by way
of a pass route near the Huerfano River, up what
is now called South Oak Creek. Governor de Anza
named this route Sangre de Cristo Pass. Sangre
de Cristo Pass, which the Ute Indians knew of
long before de Anza found it, was to remain an
important route for another century. The Spanish

Roadside aspen below Pass
Creek Pass.

built a small dirt fort on the east side of the pass in 1819, and Captain John Gunnison hauled his wagons over the pass in 1853 in search of railroad routes to California. Sangre de Cristo Pass was also used as one of the supply routes into the booming Silverton area in the mid 1870s until the Denver and Rio Grande Railway offered a better route via La Veta Pass.

Near the summit of Sangre de Cristo Pass, another pass trail branched off to the north. This route, known as Pass Creek Pass, led down the Pass Creek drainage into the Huerfano River valley and then to the Wet Mountain Valley, between the Sangre de Cristos and the Wet Mountains. Today, the Sangre de Cristo Pass route no longer exists on the east side except as a hiking trail, but the Pass Creek trail has grown to a smoothly graded automobile road between the Huerfano Valley and US Highway 160 west of North La Veta Pass. Local discussion on the precise location of the dirt fort built in 1819 still persists today in Huerfano County, but the answer lies lost in the mists of history.

The route to Pass Creek Pass from the north has changed little in more than a century. From Gardner the road runs west along the Huerfano Valley road, which is also the route to Mosca Pass. About five miles up this beautiful valley, a side road to the left (Huerfano County 9) travels south through an area of lovely Spanish ranches, then begins to climb slowly up Pass Creek, where the huge cottonwoods that predominated below are replaced by stands of aspen and pine. At the summit, about twenty miles from Gardner, the Spanish Peaks rise in the distance, and US Highway 160 can be seen winding its way to the top of North La Veta Pass along the same route that the old Sangre de Cristo Pass followed.

Since the Pass Creek Pass road branches off from the Mosca Pass road, the discussion of side roads and hiking trails in the Mosca Pass area applies equally well to Pass Creek Pass. In addition, a network of side roads interconnects between the Huerfano Valley (Mosca Pass) road and the Pass Creek road. Huerfano County 9 is the direct route, but the Pass Creek Pass road can also be reached by way of Huerfano County 10 at Red Wing and from several other routes that wind through the lovely south side of the Huerfano Valley. All of these back routes cross private property, however, and many of them dead-end at local ranches, so inquire locally to avoid trespassing.

Route finding along the main branch of the Pass Creek road is not difficult, since the road is well marked at both ends and at least at one point along the route. From US Highway 160, the Pass Creek Pass road starts about two miles west of the North La Veta Pass summit. A mile east of the entrance road to old La Veta Pass, a large highway department sign marks the location.

14 La Veta Passes

Location: between Walsenburg and Fort Garland
Difficulty: open to all motor vehicles
Scenic Quality: pretty countryside with a good view of the Spanish Peaks
Historic Interest: moderate
Side Roads: several of interest
High Point: 9,382 feet
Maps: USFS map of San Isabel National Forest at 1:125,000
USGS sheet 1 of Huerfano County at 1:50,000
USGS sheet 1 of Costilla County at 1:50,000

In 1870, the Denver and Rio Grande Railway obtained a charter to construct a railroad line from Denver to El Paso, Texas, in anticipation of eventually laying tracks all the way to Mexico City. The D&RG first built a narrow gauge (three-foot width rather than the standard four-foot, eight-inch width) line to Pueblo with a branch south to the coalfields in the Trinidad area. But at this point, General Palmer and the D&RG undertook a major change in plans. El Paso was still a long way off, and the discovery of rich silver deposits in the San Juans and elsewhere to the west promised substantial passenger and freight revenues, which could in turn be used to further the D&RG's ambitious plans.

In consequence, General Palmer turned his railroad west, toward the San Luis Valley. The D&RG survey crews could have headed up the Huerfano River toward Sangre de Cristo Pass, where Captain Gunnison had struggled with his wagon train nearly a quarter century earlier. Instead, Palmer's railroadmen selected a somewhat more southerly route down the Cucharas River. The Hayden *Atlas of 1877* shows the D&RG line ending at the town of La Veta, which the track crews had reached the previous year. From La Veta, the route ran northwestward up a steep

The Spanish Peaks from La Veta Pass.

grade to the 9,382-foot summit of La Veta Pass and then down to Sangre de Cristo Creek, which was the route of the old Sangre de Cristo Pass road and is now the modern highway route (US 160) on the west side of the Sangre de Cristos.

But La Veta Pass did not remain a rail route for long. In 1890, the D&RG relocated the Sangre de Cristo crossing to a new pass seven miles south of La Veta Pass and due west from the town of La Veta. The new crossing, over what had been called Wagon Creek Pass, provided a lower and more direct route into the San Luis Valley and Alamosa. Wagon Creek Pass was renamed Veta Pass, and the old La Veta Pass route became a wagon road. With the arrival of the automotive era, the La Veta Pass road was upgraded to a modern highway. Yet the complex story of La Veta Pass does not end here. In the early 1960s, the Colorado Highway Department selected a more direct and slightly higher alignment to replace the original La Veta Pass highway. This new alignment, which crosses the Sangre de Cristos about one and one-half miles farther to the north, became North La Veta Pass; it is the present route of US Highway 160. In consequence, there are three related pass routes: the original railroad and initial highway route (La Veta Pass), the modern rail route (Veta Pass), and the modern highway route (North La Veta Pass).

The old La Veta Pass route, abandoned when the new highway opened, is now a scenic and rarely used byroad that offers a relaxing and enjoyable alternative to the North La Veta Pass road. The old route, which is a five-mile stretch of deteriorated highway, travels to the south of the main road through lightly wooded ranching country that offers scenes of quiet beauty and a magnificent view of the Spanish Peaks rising to the southeast. On the east side of North La Veta Pass, the old road begins about two miles below the pass summit at the Muleshoe, which allowed the old railroad route to snake around the steep back side of Dump Mountain. The route continues over the gentle pass summit, travels by an abandoned settlement, then rejoins the main highway about two and one-half miles west of North La Veta Pass and one-half mile below the exit to Pass Creek Pass.

In addition to the Pass Creek Pass road, several other scenic side routes are available in the area. The modern highway route (US 160), unlike the old railroad route, bypasses the town of La Veta. Travelers who wish to enjoy a more leisurely route can exit on State Highway 12 or the more scenic and unpaved Valley Road, for a visit to the old La Veta cemetery and the charming town of La Veta before rejoining US 160. From the north edge of La Veta, a road of deteriorating quality appears to travel up Indian Creek to the San Isabel National Forest boundary and over an unnamed Sangre de Cristo crossing into Costilla County (*see* No. 62, No Name Pass). From La Veta, additional and better-maintained roads travel south past dramatic Goemmer Butte, a volcanic plug, and into the magnificent countryside of the Cucharas River valley below the flanks of East and West Spanish Peaks.

15 Apishapa (or Cordova) Pass

Location: between Aguilar on Interstate 25
and Cucharas Pass on Colorado Highway 12
Difficulty: can be negotiated by most smaller
passenger cars under good conditions
Scenic Quality: very scenic area with excellent
views of the Spanish Peaks
Historic Interest: slight
Side Roads: several of interest
High Point: 11,248 feet
Maps: USFS map of San Isabel National
Forest at 1:125,000
USGS sheet 4 of Las Animas County at 1:50,000
USGS sheet 4 of Huerfano County at 1:50,000
Colorado highway map at 1:1,000,000

Apishapa Pass is not technically a Sangre de
Cristo crossing but a pass route over the high
ridge that extends east from the Sangre de Cristo
Range and is capped by the Spanish Peaks. The
pass route follows the Apishapa (Apache for
"stinking water") River west to its headwaters
just below West Spanish Peak, crosses the ridge
at a gentle gap, and winds down about 1,000 vertical feet to Cucharas Pass, located above the
headwaters of the Cucharas and Apishapa rivers.

The Apishapa Pass route was known and
used periodically in the nineteenth century and
probably had seen centuries of prior travel by
Spanish traders and nomadic Indians. But today
the modern pass road is a little known and charming backcountry route through a rarely visited
area. As an additional bonus, the route provides a
series of outstanding opportunities to view close-
up the Spanish Peaks from their rarely seen south
side.

From the east, the road to Apishapa Pass begins at Aguilar, a peaceful town located just west
of Interstate 25 between Walsenburg and Trinidad. At the southwest end of Aguilar, a paved
road leads up a lovely Spanish farming valley to

Stone archway on the Apishapa Pass road.

Gulnare, beyond which the Apishapa Road forks to the right. The road continues up the valley with the Spanish Peaks coming into increasingly close view on the north. The pass road then climbs into deserted forests of aspen and pine and travels through a picturesque stone arch built through a volcanic dike by Civilian Conservation Corps work crews in 1940. Near the summit of Apishapa Pass unfold excellent views of West Spanish Peak, and from the summit ridge, which the Forest Service sign labels as Cordova Pass, the Sangre de Cristos rise proudly above the gently rolling meadows and pine forests that dominate the west side of the pass. A winding descent about five miles in length ends at the summit of Cucharas Pass on Colorado Highway 12. Colorado 12 north of Cucharas Pass leads to the Cucharas Valley Ski Area and sweeping scenic vistas; Colorado 12 south of the pass travels an equally scenic route through Stonewall Gap and the community of Stonewall.

On the east side of Apishapa Pass, several side roads lead off both to the north and the south along the network of small canyons and valleys east of the Culebra Range. A side road to the north along Trujillo Creek leads into National Forest lands and the hiking trails that give access to the Spanish Peaks. On the west side of the pass road are no side roads of interest. However, about ten miles south of Cucharas Pass on Colorado Highway 12, a side road travels from Monument Park up Whiskey Creek and along a tributary drainage toward a very high Sangre de Cristo crossing into the San Luis Valley. This Whiskey Pass route, some 12,500 feet high, was a depression era Works Progress Administration (WPA) project that was never completed. The ambitious plans called for a tunnel crossing at the 12,000-foot level. The pass route is located entirely on privately owned land within the Maxwell Grant and consequently is closed to public access.

A view of East Spanish Peak from the Apishapa Pass road.

The Blue River Valley and the Gore Range from the Ute Pass road.

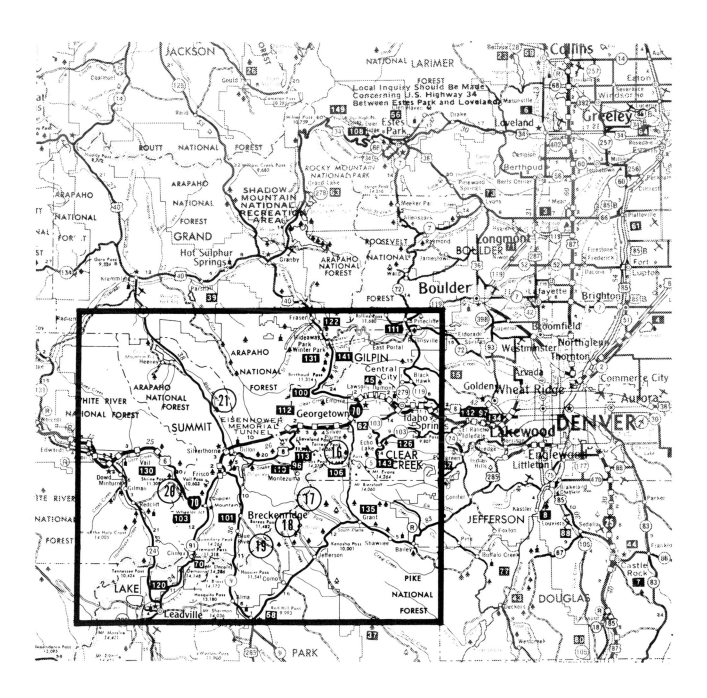

Part Three
Summit County Passes

For eons of time the Blue River Valley lay dormant, blocked on three sides by high mountain walls penetrated only by the Indians and a few mountain men. The commercial impetus for the settlement of Summit County, one of the original seventeen territorial counties of Colorado, occurred in the summer of 1859 with the discovery of placer gold in the Blue River Valley near the site of Breckenridge. By 1860, thousands of prospectors were swarming over the Continental Divide at Boreas Pass (then Breckenridge Pass) and Georgia Pass in search of gold.

Soon after the first discoveries of placer gold, rich lodes of silver and gold were located along Saints John Creek and Peru Creek in the Montezuma area, east of Breckenridge. Initially, no practical route could be found to transport the ore, although many of the mine sites lay less than ten miles from Georgetown. The tall backbone of the Continental Divide stood in the way of a direct route. The Argentine Pass road, opened in 1871, was too high and steep a route into Montezuma for regular commercial traffic. So the Montezuma Silver Mining Company pioneered a new road over the Continental Divide and down the Hall Valley on the east side of Kenosha Pass. This new route, opened in 1878, was called Webster Pass. It provided a direct link with Denver.

A year later, the Montezuma area obtained direct access to Georgetown when William Loveland opened his pass road north of the Argentine road; this new route traveled from Denver and Georgetown to Montezuma, the Breckenridge-Frisco area, and on to the silver mines of Leadville. In 1882, the Denver, South Park, and Pacific Railroad opened a narrow gauge rail line over Boreas Pass, into the Frisco area, and over Fremont Pass to Leadville. With the discovery of gold and silver on McClellan Mountain, near Argentine Pass, a railroad line was extended from Georgetown along the Argentine Pass road almost to the Continental Divide.

The Silver Panic of 1893 and the exhaustion of Summit County's placer and lode mines brought to a close the heyday of most early Summit County pass roads. Loveland, Hoosier, and Fremont passes survived to become major thoroughfares, but the others slipped into obscurity. So, too, did the towns of Summit County die down. In 1877, the Princeton Scientific Expedition had noted, "We heartily recommend Breckenridge as being the most fiendish place we ever wish to visit." By 1910, the population of Breckenridge had dropped to 834 and its fiendish ways had become only a memory. Not until the 1960s, which brought the creation of Dillon Reservoir and the birth of major skiing areas in Summit County, did Breckenridge, Frisco, and other communities in the area regain a semblance of their past glory.

The mountain passes of western Summit County are less well known or are of more recent origin than those along the southern and eastern rims of the county. Shrine Pass, which dates back to the later days of the nineteenth century, was for many years the direct route through Summit County to Glenwood Springs and Grand Junction. It allowed travellers to bypass the lengthier route over Fremont Pass to Leadville and then over Tennessee Pass or over Independence Pass to Glenwood Springs. Kokomo Pass, now only a hiking trail, served the once thriving mines in the Kokomo area in southwest Summit County, which reportedly housed some 10,000 miners during a brief boom.

Vail Pass, which spans the Gore Range between Tenmile Creek on the east and Gore Creek to the west, was not built until 1940. Prior to that time, Red Buffalo Pass, about six miles east of Silverthorne, provided access to the Gore Valley. In the 1960s, Red Buffalo Pass received serious consideration for the Interstate highway route over the Gore Mountains, but the Colorado Highway Department instead selected the already developed but much longer corridor along Tenmile Creek and over Vail Pass.

16 Argentine Pass

Location: between Georgetown on Interstate 70 and Montezuma, off US Highway 40
Difficulty: four-wheel-drive required to reach the summit
Scenic Quality: outstanding alpine scenery
Historic Interest: very high
High Point: 13,207 feet
Side Roads: several of considerable interest
Maps: USFS map of Arapaho National Forest at 1:125,000
USGS sheet 2 of Summit County at 1:50,000
USGS single sheet of Clear Creek County at 1:50,000

The motivation for construction of a road from Georgetown over Argentine Pass lay in the rich gold and silver deposits above Peru Creek and the Snake River basin. Though less than ten miles from Georgetown, these ore deposits were separated from civilization by a massive, 13,000-foot-high ridge of the Continental Divide.

This situation was remedied, at least temporarily, by "Commodore" Stephen Decatur, a renegade eastern aristocrat with many talents and several wives. Decatur was not only a Williams College graduate and a road builder, but an Indian fighter, Mexican War hero, mining man of vision, city planner, and later a Colorado senator. Decatur's daring toll road over Argentine Pass, completed in 1871, still ranks as the highest pass road ever constructed over the Continental Divide. Unfortunately for Decatur, the towering summit and narrow, terrifying descent down the west side of the pass doomed the Argentine road to commercial failure. Wind, snow, and rock slides frequently prevented the passage of man or beast over the road and led to abandonment of the route in favor of more sane if less direct routes into the silver mines above Montezuma.

The most famous historical site along the

The Argentine Pass road. Note the older corduroy road in the foreground and the modern route in the near background.

40

Argentine road is the town of Waldorf, established above timberline on the east side of the pass beside rich deposits of silver ore that were first mined in 1867. The town once included a boardinghouse, hotel, fifty-ton ore mill, stables, machine shops, and the highest post office (at 11,666 feet) in the nation. Development of the Waldorf mines was promoted by an energetic Methodist minister, Edward John Wilcox, who reportedly decided that the interests of his religion would be better served by tithing his own wealth than preaching the gospel.

In 1906, Reverend Wilcox completed the Argentine Central Railway to link Waldorf with Silver Plume and Georgetown. The narrow gauge line not only hauled out ore, but also brought trainloads of tourists to Waldorf and McClellan Mountain, where sightseers could marvel at the view, gawk at the "ice caves" (actually ice-lined mine shafts), or explore the nearby site of an attempted railroad tunnel underneath the Divide. *Clason's Colorado Hotel Guide and Commercial Index* for 1909 raved: "The trip up Clear Creek Canyon to Idaho Springs, Georgetown and Silver Plume via the Colorado & Southern Ry.; thence to the summit of Mt. McClellan, by way of the Argentine Central Ry., where one may enjoy the unique experience of snowballing in summer is without doubt the grandest scenic trip in Colorado."

The well-graded, present-day Argentine Pass road begins on the Guanella Pass road above Georgetown and climbs gently through the woods to Waldorf. Most passenger cars can negotiate the road to Waldorf, but no farther. Beyond Waldorf, the road ascends a rough and occasionally steep route above timberline to the breathtaking top of the pass. From there, modern-day travelers can look or hike—but not drive—down the narrow shelf road that Stephan Decatur carved into the side of the Continental Divide.

Route finding in the Argentine Pass area presents no difficulties. The Guanella Pass road begins prominently at the south end of Georgetown, and the Argentine Pass road starts at a large but unmarked turnoff about three miles up the Guanella Pass road. The Waldorf area includes several scenic side roads. Just before Waldorf, a four-wheel-drive road descends into the valley, affording excellent summertime picnic sites among the wild flowers in the meadow. Another four-wheel-drive road from the edge of Waldorf (do not take the road straight up, which ends in a bog) ascends McClellan Mountain, ending on a high ridge. A brief walk to the ridge line yields an awesome view of Stephens Gulch, nearly 2,000 feet below, from which Grays and Torreys peaks rise abruptly. A hike along the rock-strewn ridge leads to the 14,270-foot summit of Grays Peak, only 1,200 vertical feet above the end of the McClellan Mountain road.

The west side access to Argentine Pass, briefly described in the following section on Webster Pass, begins on the west side of the Webster Pass road and ascends Peru Creek, from the upper portion of which visitors can view—or climb—the long, exposed shelf road, now littered with rock debris, to the summit of Argentine Pass.

17 Webster Pass

Location: between US Highway 6 at the
Keystone ski area and US Highway 285 at
Webster
Difficulty: safe ascent on the east side
requires a narrow-track four-wheel-drive
vehicle/caution recommended
Scenic Quality: attractive scenery on the
west side with imposing summit view
Historic Interest: very high
Side Roads: various of exceptional historic
and scenic value
High Point: 12,096 feet
Maps: USFS map of Arapaho National Forest
at 1:125,000
USGS sheet 2 of Summit County at 1:50,000
USGS sheet 1 of Park County at 1:50,000

Originally called Handcart Pass, this route
over the Continental Divide was renamed
Webster Pass by the Webster brothers, who constructed a toll road along the route in 1878 in co-
operation with the Montezuma Silver Mining
Company. Built for hauling freight and passengers to the Peru Creek and Snake River area, the
road was heavily traveled until the decline of the
once rich mines above Montezuma.

The Webster Pass road leads from the town
of Montezuma up the Snake River to a wide
valley and over the Divide to Handcart Gulch and
then down Hall Valley to the abandoned town
site of Webster, beside US Highway 285. The
west side of the road winds smoothly and sceni-
cally to the top of the pass, affording a magnificent view of nearby Red Cone Peak. From the
summit, which can be reached from the west
without four-wheel-drive, the road makes a spectacular descent along a narrow, bumpy, and occasionally off-camber shelf for several miles. Considerable caution and a narrow-track vehicle are
required for safe descent to the valley. Below timberline, the road cuts through a lovely forest,
passing beside the remains of a once thriving dis-

The east side route to Webster Pass. The foreground sign offers good advice. The background sign incorrectly
announces that this is a dead-end road.

The barren but spectacular Webster Pass shelf road.

trict of mines and abandoned buildings. In its heyday, the Hall Valley and Handcart Gulch area reportedly contained a population of several hundred ill-behaved miners.

Route finding in the Webster Pass area is not an easy task, since few signs indicate the road. From the west, take the Montezuma road (Summit County Road 5) at the Keystone ski area, beside US Highway 40, travel through Montezuma, and turn left at Summit County Road 285, a mile beyond Montezuma. The road travels up the Snake River valley, and about two and one-half miles later, a road bears left for the ascent to Webster Pass. The top of the pass is readily visible from the valley below. From the east, take US Highway 285 to Webster and turn north at Park County Road 60, ignoring the Forest Service sign that declares this to be a dead-end road. The route up Hall Valley bears to the right, along Handcart Gulch. The southern fork of the road continues up Hall Valley, ending dramatically in a high cirque above the headwaters of the North Fork of the South Platte River.

The west side of Webster Pass offers several outstanding side trips. The main branch of the Montezuma road leads up Deer Creek into the Radical Hill area, and another branch of the Montezuma road, slightly below the town of Montezuma, travels up Peru Creek to Horseshoe Basin. This high valley, the site of an historic mining district, sits at the foot of Argentine Pass, encircled by a ring of stunning 13,000-foot and 14,000-foot peaks.

From the Snake River valley road, at the Webster Pass turnoff, another road continues up the valley, passing through an area of extraordinary beauty, then steeply ascends Teller Mountain onto a high ridge overlooking a vast expanse of mountainous terrain. A road traverses the length of the ridge. To the north it passes the

still-standing remains of the General Teller mine and then descends steeply down Glacier Mountain to Saints John, a picturesque and once thriving company mining town. This road then continues more gently along the creek to Montezuma and US Highway 6 at the foot of Loveland Pass.

To the south, the high ridge road crosses to Swandyke, another abandoned mining area, and descends the scenic Middle Fork of the Swan River to Tiger road (Summit County Road 6), which ends at Colorado Highway 9, about three miles north of Breckenridge. Near the abandoned town site of Parkville, the Georgia Pass road down the South Fork of the Swan River (*see* Georgia Pass) also joins the Tiger road. Consequently, an adventuresome traveler from US Highway 285 can use this route from Webster Pass to cross the Continental Divide once again and return to US 285 at Jefferson. Since numerous unmarked roads crosscut the Parkville area, trial and error is sometimes required to locate the South Fork road.

Both of these side trips above the Snake River rank among the most spectacular backcountry excursions in Colorado. However, they should be undertaken with caution and only by experienced travelers, in good weather and with proper equipment. The road up Teller Mountain, which is steep and exposed, opens onto an alpine ridge that offers no protection from the elements. The descent both to Montezuma and Breckenridge includes precipitous stretches of road that are challenging even for experienced trail bike riders and four-wheel-drive operators. Nor are existing maps of much use in the area. Neither the U.S. Geologic Survey topographic maps nor the Forest Service maps indicate the main road or the several side roads branching off in various directions, and not a single road sign exists along the entire route.

18 Georgia Pass

Location: between US Highway 285 at Jefferson and Colorado Highway 9 north of Breckenridge

Difficulty: four-wheel-drive required for travel on the west side; most passenger cars can ascend the east side

Scenic Quality: nice summit views; best scenery on the west side

Historic Interest: very high

Side Roads: various of considerable interest

High Point: 11,585 feet

Maps: USFS map of Arapaho National Forest at 1:125,000

USGS sheet 2 of Summit County at 1:50,000

USGS sheet 1 of Park County at 1:50,000

On returning from California in 1844, Lieutenant John Fremont led his second expedition through North Park, Middle Park, and up the Blue River by the future site of Breckenridge in search of new routes over the Rockies. Because Arapaho warriors were traveling along a pass trail up the Swan River, Fremont decided to continue along the Blue River and cross Hoosier Pass into South Park.

With the discovery of gold near Breckenridge in 1859, miners by the thousands swarmed over the Continental Divide and down the Swan River route that Fremont had wisely avoided fifteen summers earlier. The Georgia Pass trail soon widened into a wagon road that could accommodate supplies and equipment. Eventually, the smoother grade at Hoosier Pass and Boreas Pass led to the abandonment of Georgia Pass, but for several years Georgia Pass served as a chief route into the booming Breckenridge area. The Hayden Survey for 1873 noted that the grade on both sides of the pass was "easy" and that a wagon road of indifferent quality crossed the pass.

On the east side, the Georgia Pass road begins on US Highway 285 at Jefferson and gently ascends for 2,000 feet to a flat summit that

Mount Guyot from the Georgia Pass road.

Mount Guyot from the summit of Georgia Pass.

affords a striking view of South Park and Mt. Guyot directly to the west. Most passenger cars can reach the pass summit from US Highway 285 in South Park. The more scenic west side of the road, however, is steep, narrow, and rough for a two-mile stretch below the summit. Only four-wheel-drive vehicles should attempt this portion of the trip.

The Georgia Pass road is not well marked. On the east side, take Park County Road 35 at Jefferson and continue on this road toward Michigan Creek for nearly three miles, bearing right at Park County Road 54. At the summit of the pass, a side road leads to the east along a ridge line, and another side road traverses to the west, ending just beyond an imposing flank of Mt. Guyot. The main road, which appears less well traveled than the side route to the west, descends straight downhill, entering a maze of side roads about five miles below the summit and exiting onto Summit County Road 354 and thence to Tiger road (Summit County Road 6). The west side approach follows State Highway 9 to Tiger road about three and one-half miles north of Breckenridge, then proceeds to Summit County Road 354 and up the South Fork of the Swan River or, alternately, up the Middle Fork road a short distance with a right-hand turn onto the main route.

On the east side of Georgia Pass, a scenic alternate route travels up French Creek and joins the main road near the top of the pass. Several additional side roads exist in the South Fork valley, and in the Parkville area is an abundance of secondary roads that lead to abandoned mining sites.

For the adventurous traveler, a thrilling side road (*see also* Webster Pass) leads up the Middle Fork of the Swan River, past the Swandyke mining site, and along a lengthy traverse above timberline to Glacier Mountain and then down to Saints John and Montezuma or, alternately, down Teller Mountain into the upper Snake River valley. The main road through the Snake River valley also leads to Montezuma or, alternately, over Webster Pass and back to US Highway 285 at Webster. This spectacular double pass trip, which takes most of a day to complete by motor vehicle, returns to the highway less than ten miles from the starting point.

Travelers who elect to try these magnificent side trips up the Middle Fork of the Swan River should heed the cautions included in the description of Webster Pass. The area between Swandyke and Saints John is exposed alpine terrain; the roads are largely unmapped and include extremely steep, rough, and narrow stretches that even well-equipped four-wheel-drive vehicles may have difficulty negotiating. Travel in this area should be undertaken only by experienced mountain travelers in good weather and with adequate equipment.

19 Boreas Pass

Location: between Breckenridge and US
   Highway 285 at Como
Difficulty: can be traversed by most
   passenger cars under good conditions
Scenic Quality: attractive area with good
   summit views
Historic Interest: very high
Side Roads: several of historic interest
High Point: 11,481 feet
Maps: USFS map of Arapaho National Forest
   at 1:125,000
USGS sheet 2 of Summit County at 1:50,000
USGS sheet 1 of Park County at 1:50,000
Colorado highway map at 1:1,000,000

Immediately following the discovery of gold
near Breckenridge in 1859, miners by the thousands came rushing over the Continental Divide
at Georgia Pass and Breckenridge Pass. Within a
year, the Breckenridge Pass road was widened to
accommodate wagons and then stagecoaches. In
1882, Sidney Dillon, who ran the Union Pacific
Railway, had begun laying tracks up Breckenridge Pass, which he renamed Boreas Pass in
honor of the Greek god of the north wind. The
railroad grade was steep and windswept, but it
gave the UP's subsidiary railroad, the Denver,
South Park, and Pacific, access to Leadville even
if it required topping two passes (Boreas and Fremont), each more than 11,000 feet high. At one
time, the Boreas Pass rail line was the highest in
the country; the route over the summit included
nearly a dozen snowsheds and grades in excess of
4 percent. After the tracks were abandoned in
1937, the Army Corps of Engineers reconstructed
the route for automobile travel.

Various historic features remain along this
famous route. At the summit is the abandoned
town of Boreas, now in ruins, and on the west
side, the famous Baker water tank has been restored to a semblance of its original condition.
The route up the pass from the east begins on US
Highway 285 at Como. Take Park County Road
33 and follow the various Boreas Pass road signs

The former town site of Boreas after a fall snowstorm.

Modern day Breckenridge from the Boreas Pass road.

to the summit. The east side of the road includes a few rough spots that might cause difficulty for low-slung passenger cars, but the traveler is rewarded with attractive stands of aspen and a good view of Mt. Silverheels. The Boreas Pass road is a favorite fall route for aspen watchers. The west side of the road, which begins at the south end of Breckenridge from Colorado Highway 9, is smooth and wide. It climbs gently to the summit, traversing a lovely forest. To the west, the high peaks of the Tenmile Range are visible.

Several scenic side roads branch off from the Boreas Pass road. On the east side, about three and one-half miles from the highway, well-used side roads lead up Tarryall and North Tarryall creeks, and additional routes allow a traveler to explore the smaller drainages. The Tarryall Creek area once housed a flourishing community of miners. The Hayden Survey report for 1873 placed the peak population of Tarryall, near the head of the creek, at 2,000 to 3,000 persons but noted that the number of residents had declined to 200.

On the west side of Boreas Pass, a road down Indiana Creek leads to the site of Dyersville and several abandoned mines. Dyersville, which flourished briefly in the early 1880s, was named for Father Dyer. The famous itinerant preacher of Mosquito Pass fame reportedly established and later sold a mining claim located at this site in order to help finance his ministerial travels.

20 Shrine Pass

Location: between Vail Pass on Interstate 70 and Redcliffe on US Highway 24
Difficulty: can be traversed by most smaller passenger cars under good conditions
Scenic Quality: very attractive, gentle countryside
Historic Interest: modest
Side Roads: several of high scenic value
High Point: 11,089 feet
Maps: USFS map of Arapaho National Forest at 1:125,000
USFS map of White River National Forest at 1:125,000
USGS sheet 2 of Summit County at 1:50,000
USGS sheet 4 of Eagle County at 1:50,000
Colorado highway map at 1:1,000,000

This once popular route west to Glenwood Springs and Grand Junction fell into disuse when the US Highway 6 route over Loveland Pass was extended up West Tenmile Creek and into the Gore Valley over a pass route several miles southeast of Shrine Pass. The new road, opened in 1940, was modestly named in honor of Charles Vail, a highway engineer who had advocated the route.

The Shrine Pass road, now maintained by the Forest Service, has become a scenic route from the summit of Vail Pass to the town of Redcliff on US Highway 24. The road traverses a series of lovely meadows and pine-filled woodlands and gently descends down Turkey Creek to the old mining sites around Redcliff. Distant but magnificent views of Mount of the Holy Cross are

Telephoto view of Mount of the Holy Cross from the west side of Shrine Pass.

available from several points along the road, and the meadows are alive with wild flowers in the summer. On the west side of the pass, scenic side roads branch off at Lime Creek, Timber Creek, and Hank's Gulch.

The Shrine Pass road is a popular sightseeing area in fall and an even more popular winter sports recreation site that receives heavy use by snowmobilers and cross-country skiers. The cross-country ski trip over Shrine Pass ranks among the most memorable ski tours in Colorado. Following a lengthy car shuttle from Vail Pass to Redcliff, skiers ascend by Shrine Pass for a mile, then enjoy a downhill run of nearly ten miles through powder-filled valleys and down the gently sloping road to Redcliff. The trip is best accomplished following a heavy snowfall to ensure an adequate base on the lower portion of the road.

Route finding in the Shrine Pass area presents few difficulties. From the east, take Exit 190 on Interstate 70 at the top of Vail Pass and proceed due west. To approach Shrine Pass from the west, take US Highway 24 to Redcliff and turn east in the center of town at the sign pointing the way to Shrine Pass.

Another view of Holy Cross from the west side of Shrine Pass.

21 Ute Pass

Location: between Fraser at US Highway 40 and Colorado Highway 9 north of Interstate 70

Difficulty: traversable by most smaller passenger cars under good conditions

Scenic Quality: nice countryside in Williams Fork area

Historic Interest: slight

Side Roads: several of moderate interest

High Point: 9,524 feet

Maps: USFS map of Arapaho National Forest at 1:125,000

USGS sheet 1 of Summit County at 1:50,000

USGS sheets 3 and 4 of Grand County at 1:50,000

Originally an Indian trail, this low pass road over the Williams Fork Mountains connects the scenic Fraser Valley by the foot of Rollins Pass with the Blue River valley north of Breckenridge and Dillon. Although Ute Pass does not rank among the most spectacular features of the Colorado landscape, the pass road traverses an uncrowded and very scenic area.

From the west, a broad, smooth road of recent origin quickly ascends the pass and drops into the Williams Fork Valley, skirting AMAX's huge Henderson molybdenum mine. From the Williams Fork River, the road travels north for slightly more than two miles to the Horseshoe Campground. The north fork of the road continues to the Williams Fork Reservoir and Kremmling on US Highway 40, while the east branch crosses a scenic vantage point and several inviting meadows along the way to Fraser, also on US Highway 40. On this eastern portion of the road, in the Church Park area, some passenger cars may experience difficulty, depending on the road conditions and available ground clearance.

Despite these minor difficulties, the route

Winter view of the Gore Range from the Ute Pass road.

Winter scene along the Williams Fork River.

makes a pleasant excursion by itself or in conjunction with a trip over Rollins Pass. The Williams Fork area holds a sizable population of deer, elk, smaller animals, and a diverse assortment of birds. One summer afternoon several years ago, while lounging on a broad meadow beside the pass road, I watched in fascination through my field glasses as a coyote tracked back and forth along the far edge of the meadow trying to pick up a scent it could not quite locate.

Route finding along the Ute Pass road presents few difficulties. On the west side, the pass road begins on Colorado Highway 9, about twelve and one-half miles north of the I-70 Silverthorne exit, at Summit County Road 15. The approach from Fraser is not so straightforward, since several other roads go west from town. Proceed west from Fraser, avoiding the Saint Louis Creek road to the Byers Creek Campground, then turn

south at the Horseshoe Campground onto the Williams Fork road and proceed for slightly more than two miles south before turning to the west.

Failure to turn at this junction south of the campground will result in a lovely six-mile side trip along the Williams Fork road to the South Fork and Sugarloaf campgrounds. This route passes beneath the right-of-way for AMAX's electric powered narrow gauge railroad, which is used to haul ore between the Henderson mine and the crushing mill located by the foot of Jones Pass. From the South Fork Campground, a hiking trail travels to Saint Louis Pass. From the Sugarloaf Campground, another trail leads to the Bobtail mine by the base of Jones Pass.

The Williams Fork route offers several other side roads farther to the north, and additional, more primitive side roads exist in the Church Park area, about twelve miles west of Fraser.

August storm clouds on Mt. Massive, Sawatch Range.

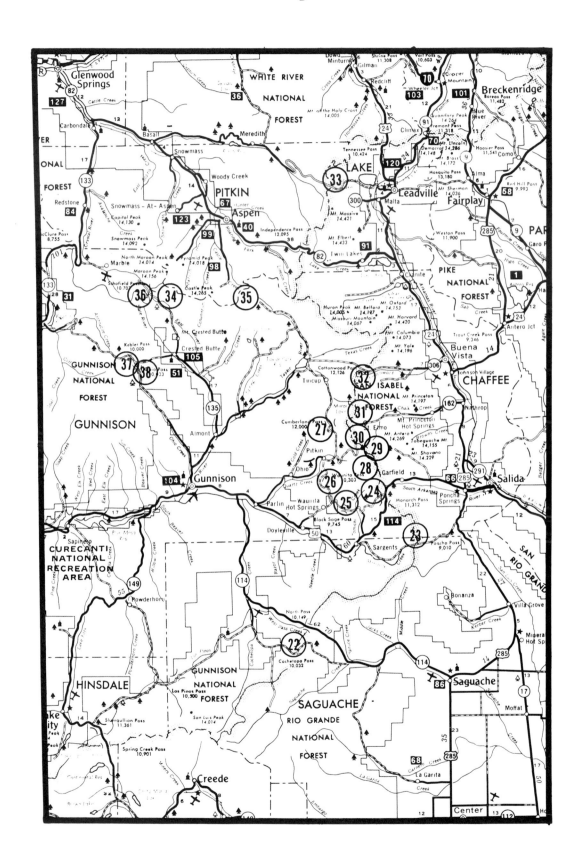

Part Four
Gunnison Country and
Sawatch Passes

On June 23, 1853, Captain John Gunnison of the U.S. Topographic Engineers began a well-financed government expedition between the thirty-eighth and thirty-ninth parallels in search of a railroad route over the Rockies to California. Gunnison's entourage of soldiers and scientists traveled past Bent's Fort in eastern Colorado, explored Medano Pass and Mosca Pass, crossed Poncha Pass, and traveled over Cochetopa Pass to the Gunnison River and then down the Colorado River into Utah. South of Salt Lake City, Indians attacked Gunnison and his party, who became the innocent victims of a feud between the Mormons and local bands of Paiute Indians. The ensuing massacre, in which Gunnison and all but four members of the expedition were killed, ranked as the worst such disaster to befall an army surveying expedition in the West.

Captain Gunnison's memory was, however, well preserved: his name lives on in the form of Gunnison County, the town of Gunnison, Mt. Gunnison, the Gunnison River, and Gunnison Reservoir in Utah near the site of his death. These place names are a fitting tribute to the West Point soldier turned explorer for pass routes. Gunnison County, like Summit County, is rimmed more than halfway around its circumference by high mountain ranges, yet it is a natural gateway. Once the traveler overcomes these mountain barriers, a river valley leads downstream to Grand Junction and the confluence with the Colorado River, while other routes travel southwest to the San Juans and beyond.

As a land of historically important and visually impressive gateways, Gunnison County is rivaled only by the San Juans. At the eastern border of the county, along the Continental Divide and neighboring ranges, more than a half dozen high pass routes (Lake Pass, Cottonwood Pass, Tincup Pass, Williams Pass, Hancock Pass, the Monarch passes, Marshall Pass, and Cochetopa Pass) lead into Gunnison County. Four additional passes—Cumberland, Tomichi, Black Sage, and Waunita—interconnect the once thriving and still scenic Gunnison country mining towns

situated to the west of the Continental Divide. McClure Pass, Schofield Pass, East Maroon Pass, Conundrum and Triangle passes, Pearl Pass, and Taylor Pass lead over the magnificent Elk Range, along the northern border of Gunnison County. Ohio Pass traverses a low but lovely mountain range between the cities of Gunnison and Crested Butte, and Kebler Pass, a short distance away, provides access between Crested Butte and the North Fork Valley of the Gunnison River.

A number of these Elk Range pass routes are no more than faintly marked trails accessible only to strong and experienced mountain hikers. But there are sufficient pass roads throughout Gunnison County to afford two- and four-wheel-drive motorized travelers the special pleasure of circle tours with a variety of excursions down little-used byways that lead to places of high historic interest and great scenic value.

In the central and northern part of Gunnison County, a circle tour can be taken from Gunnison over Ohio Pass and Kebler Pass down to the North Fork of the Gunnison River, then over McClure Pass and up the majestic Crystal River valley to Schofield Pass and back to Gunnison by way of Gothic and Crested Butte. In eastern Gunnison County, elaborate circle trips abound. Starting in Buena Vista, a traveler can drive over Cottonwood Pass and down to Tincup, then over Cumberland Pass to Pitkin, and from there either exit the county over Hancock Pass or travel south over Waunita Pass and Black Sage Pass, leaving the county either by way of Monarch Pass or Marshall Pass.

Before travelers attempt the more strenuous of these routes, they should ensure that the capability and range of their vehicles, the local road conditions, and the limits of their own endurance are adequate to provide safe passage. Since the Gunnison County area (especially in the Elk Mountains and the Collegiate Range) includes some of the most spectacular hiking trails in Colorado, backcountry travelers should carry—and use—a route book such as Ormes' *Guide to the Colorado Mountains*.

22 Cochetopa Pass

Location: between Saguache and Gunnison
Difficulty: can be negotiated by most passenger cars under normal conditions
Scenic Quality: pretty area with open countryside and nice vistas
Historic Interest: very high
Side Roads: extensive network on both sides of pass
High Point: about 10,030 feet
Maps: USFS map of Rio Grande National Forest at 1:125,000
USFS map of Gunnison National Forest at 1:125,000
USGS sheet 1 of Saguache County at 1:50,000
Colorado highway map at 1:1,000,000

Marker at the summit of Cochetopa Pass.

Between the Gunnison River valley and the land to the east stands the Continental Divide. In the later decades of the nineteenth century, European settlers built crossings into the Gunnison country at a variety of gaps along the Divide: at Cottonwood Pass, Tincup Pass, Monarch Pass, and Marshall Pass. But the traditional points of crossing were located to the south, through the low and rolling Cochetopa Hills where the Continental Divide dips down to barely 10,000 feet in elevation. The word "cochetopa" means "pass of the buffalo" in the Ute language, and the Cochetopa Pass routes were a traditional passageway for nomadic Indian groups centuries before the arrival of European settlers in Colorado. By the early decades of the nineteenth century, not only the Utes but also Spanish traders, trappers, and other early explorers were making extensive use of the Cochetopa Pass trails.

In the 1820s, Antoine Robidoux took pack trains over Mosca Pass and Cochetopa Pass on his way west to Utah. In 1848, Lieutenant John Fremont attempted to scout a railroad route over Cochetopa Pass, but winter storms halted his progress at a site in the La Garita Mountains about eighteen miles south of the pass. Five years later, Captain Gunnison's ill-fated expedition hauled its wagons over Cochetopa Pass in search of railroad routes to California. In 1875, Otto Mears constructed a toll road over Cochetopa Pass to link his Poncha Pass toll road with Gunnison, Lake City, Silverton, and the Ute Indian territory.

Because the Cochetopa Hills offer so many crossing points, a variety of pass routes exist throughout the area. Hayden's 1877 *Atlas of Colorado* shows two different pass roads over the Cochetopa Hills. The route labeled Cochetopa

Pass by the Hayden Survey is actually North Cochetopa Pass (called North Pass on contemporary Forest Service maps), which is the route of Colorado State Highway 114 between Saguache and Gunnison. Otto Mears' toll road route goes over the Divide at a point four miles to the south at a crossing that is labeled correctly on state and Forest Service maps as Cochetopa Pass. From Colorado Highway 114 west of Saguache, Cochetopa Pass is reached by way of Saguache County Road 20 (Forest Service Road NN14), which travels through an area of open pine forest and pretty rock formations to a low summit where the state of Colorado has erected a bronze marker commemorating the route. On the west side, the pass road gently descends into the broad expanse of Cochetopa Park with a lovely view of the high San Juan Peaks rising above Lake City. The Cochetopa Pass road then turns north to join the North Cochetopa Pass route (Colorado Highway 114) and winds down the scenic Cochetopa Canyon to US Highway 50 about eight miles east of Gunnison.

The Cochetopa Pass area is crosscut with an extensive network of back roads. On the east side of the pass, a local road travels north from Colorado Highway 114 up Sheep Creek and Spanish Creek to cross the Continental Divide about two miles north of North Cochetopa Pass before re-joining the highway. A side road about halfway up the east side of the Cochetopa Pass road leads to several more unnamed crossings of the Continental Divide to the south of Cochetopa Pass and also leads to the network of roads through Saguache Park and the La Garita Mountains. From the west side of the Cochetopa Pass road is the branch road along Los Piños Creek leading to Los Piños Pass and Lake City. In addition, a series of roads, some but not all of which require four-wheel-drive, leads south from the Cochetopa Pass road into Cochetopa Park and the rolling mountain countryside above it.

The best-known and probably the most interesting side road in the Cochetopa Pass area begins about five and one-half miles west of the pass summit at a Forest Service sign pointing the way to Saguache Park and the Stone Cellar Campground. This reasonably good road travels south to a 10,500-foot crossing of the Continental Divide about eight miles southwest of Cochetopa Pass. The Forest Service maps do not label the crossing, but it is Salt House Pass, which was known as Carnero Pass during the nineteenth century. This pass periodically served as a route from the San Luis Valley into the Gunnison River valley. From the top of Salt House Pass, the road descends through Saguache Park to Stone Cellar Campground, then turns due south to the edge of the La Garita Wilderness. About three miles east of the road, but on the other side of the La Garita Mountains, is the site where Fremont established camp to wait out the winter storms of 1848 that kept him from reaching Cochetopa Pass.

To the south and east of Salt House Pass are three additional pass routes. About a dozen miles south and accessible only by a long hike is Half-moon Pass, a high crossing of the La Garita Mountains that leads down to Creede and Wagon Wheel Gap on the Rio Grande River. To the east of Salt House Pass are two other crossings, Moon Pass and Carnero Pass. The route from the town of La Garita, located just west of US Highway 285, up Carnero Creek and past present-day Carnero Pass, was used as an alternate route to Cochetopa Pass from the lower portions of the San Luis Valley.

The several hundred square miles of National Forest land to the south of the Cochetopa Pass road are an attractive and little used mountain recreation area. But few of the roads are marked, and many side roads wind through the area, offering ample opportunity to get thoroughly lost. Consequently, travelers who intend to explore the area should take a compass, maps, and the other equipment necessary to ensure that they do not repeat Fremont's experience (which cost the expedition nearly a dozen lives) of having to establish a remote emergency camp during a severe storm.

A fence beside the Cochetopa Pass road.

23 Marshall Pass

Location: between Poncha Springs–Salida and Sargents–Gunnison
Difficulty: can be negotiated by most smaller passenger cars under good conditions
Scenic Quality: best scenery on west side
Historic Interest: high
Side Roads: several of interest
High Point: 10,846 feet
Maps: USFS map of San Isabel National Forest at 1:125,000
USFS map of Gunnison National Forest at 1:125,000
USGS sheet 3 of Chaffee County at 1:50,000
USGS sheet 2 of Saguache County at 1:50,000

Summer view from the Marshall Pass road.

Throughout the 1870s, civilian and military survey expeditions fought among themselves and in the halls of the U.S. Congress for the legal authority and public funding to explore the West. The thousands of maps, photographs, sketches, and technical reports that issued forth from these expeditions were intended both as contributions to a growing body of scientific knowledge and as instruments of propaganda that would win the support of influential congressmen. Sometimes, rival survey parties inadvertently stumbled upon each other. Just such an embarrassing event occurred in the summer of 1873, when a party of the Hayden Survey, under the auspices of the Interior Department, accidentally encountered a division of the War Department's Army Survey, under the control of Lieutenant Wheeler, while working in the Twin Lakes area of Colorado below the summit of present-day Independence Pass.

The Wheeler Survey that year was at work simultaneously in California and in Colorado. The Colorado party was led by Lieutenant William L. Marshall, who discovered the pass that was to bear his name during the course of his summer's traveling throughout southwestern Colorado. According to the story told by Marshall Sprague in *The Great Gates*, Marshall's discovery was somewhat of an accident. While in the San Juans, Lieutenant Marshall developed a severe toothache. Rather than allow a local blacksmith to remedy the problem, he decided to return to Denver. Instead of taking Cochetopa Pass into the San Luis Valley and then Mosca Pass over the Sangre de Cristos, Marshall continued east from Gunnison up a new route and descended (probably down Poncha Creek) to the Salida area on his way to Denver and the services of a trained dentist.

Lieutenant Marshall's new and shorter route soon became an important crossing of the Conti-

nental Divide. The Hayden Survey's *1877 Atlas of Colorado* noted Marshall's discovery but showed it only as a trail between Poncha Pass and the Gunnison area. In that same year, 1877, Otto Mears, the tireless builder of high roads and railroads in Colorado, constructed a wagon route from his Poncha Pass toll road over Marshall Pass and and on to Gunnison. Mears, who eventually built 450 miles of toll roads over 15 passes, sold the Marshall Pass toll route to General Palmer of the Denver and Rio Grande Railway for $13,000. The D&RG had laid tracks over La Veta Pass in 1877 and was well on its way to completing a narrow gauge rail route over Cumbres Pass at the same time that General Palmer's work crews hastily began surveying a route over Marshall Pass. By 1881, D&RG trains were traveling over the pass into Gunnison and within several years to Montrose and up the Gunnison River valley to Grand Junction.

When the mining riches and land speculation that first fueled that expansionist growth of the D&RG began to die out, the Marshall Pass route declined in significance, but the narrow gauge route was not abandoned until 1953. However, in the years just before World War II, Marshall Pass became a contender for the new all-weather highway route between Salida and Gunnison. In time, the Colorado Highway Department selected the more direct route over Monarch Pass, dooming Marshall Pass to the status of a backcountry crossing that is no longer shown by name on official Colorado highway maps.

Today, the Marshall Pass road is a scenic byway with gentle grades cutting through miles of lightly used National Forest land. From US Highway 285, about five miles south of Poncha Springs and two miles north of the Poncha Pass summit, the road climbs past O'Haver Lake and through several short rock cuts to a long, subalpine meadow that leads to the gentle summit of Marshall Pass. From the Continental Divide, the road winds through more miles of aspen, opening on to a lush valley that leads to the town of Sargents, on US Highway 50, at the base of Monarch Pass. Several miles from Sargents, a newly constructed gravel road leads up from the Marshall Pass road to the massive Homestake mine. At the pass summit, a primitive road travels south along the Divide, and another road descends Poncha Creek and rejoins the pass road below O'Haver Lake. From the abandoned town site of Shirley, about two miles above the eastern end of the Marshall Pass road, a side road ascends Silver Creek and leads into additional routes through the backcountry.

Route finding in the Marshall Pass area presents no difficulties. On US Highway 285, turn west on Chaffee County Road 200, which is marked by a state highway department sign as Marshall Pass, and follow the road toward O'Haver Lake. From Sargents on US Highway 50, a state highway department sign and a Forest Service route marker (Road XX32) point the way.

Winter scene beside the Marshall Pass road.

24 Old Monarch Pass and Original Monarch Pass

Location: between Salida on US Highway 50 and Gunnison on US Highway 50

Difficulty: can be negotiated by most passenger cars under good conditions

Scenic Quality: nicely wooded area of rolling mountainsides

Historic Interest: moderate

Side Roads: several available

High Point: about 11,375 feet

Maps: USFS map of San Isabel National Forest at 1:125,000

USFS map of Gunnison National Forest at 1:125,000

USGS sheet 3 of Chaffee County at 1:50,000

USGS sheet 5 of Gunnison County at 1:50,000

From Salida, at the start of the upper Arkansas Valley, the way west and south is blocked by high mountains. Traditionally, explorers, traders, and miners took Poncha Pass south from the Salida area to the upper portion of the San Luis Valley, then crossed the Continental Divide at Cochetopa Pass. Although this route was the long way around, it offered the distinct advantage of relatively low crossings. Another route was available up the South Fork of the South Arkansas River. This crossing over the Divide provided more direct access but at an altitude nearly one thousand feet higher than Cochetopa Pass and some two thousand feet higher than Poncha (then known as Puncho) Pass. The Hayden *Atlas* of 1877 did not show even a trail route over this South Fork route that we now call Monarch Pass.

Mountain landscape from the summit of Old Monarch Pass.

Then, in 1878, Nicholas Creede found rich ore deposits above the eastern base of Monarch Pass, and a mining boom of considerable proportion began. Within two years, a string of towns sprang up along the South Arkansas River west of Poncha Springs: Maysville, Garfield (then called Junction City), and Monarch (originally called Chaffee City), located near the site of the limestone quarries on the present-day Monarch Pass road. Within two years, the Denver and Rio Grande railroad had built a spur line from Salida along the South Arkansas River to Monarch. The simultaneous discovery of gold and silver in the Tomichi Valley, on the western side of Monarch Pass, provided further reason for the development of a road network between the Arkansas and Gunnison drainages.

The original Monarch Pass wagon route, built in 1880, still exists, but it was replaced in the early 1920s by a new crossing of the Continental Divide at a point about one mile south and some 150 feet lower. This lower crossing is now known officially as Old Monarch Pass. It suffered the same fate as the original La Veta Pass highway (see La Veta Pass in the Sangre de Cristo passes section), which was abandoned for a neighboring route that was better suited to the needs of modern-day motoring. In 1939, Old Monarch Pass was replaced by a third crossing located about one-half mile east and some sixty feet lower. This third route, known simply as Monarch Pass, is present-day US Highway 50, a sweeping and well-banked successor to the two older routes. It is also a monument to the efforts of Charles Vail, the headstrong highway engineer who championed the route in place of an alternate crossing of the Divide about eight miles to the south at Marshall Pass.

The Old Monarch Pass road is a well-marked and nicely graded back road that begins on the east side of Monarch Pass about one-half mile above the Monarch ski area. After winding briefly through a high forest of pine, the road reaches a gentle summit with a sweeping panorama of the San Juans far to the west and the rolling mountainscape of eastern Gunnison County. From here, the road gently descends through nine miles of lovely and lightly used forest to Tomichi Creek, where it intersects a high-quality gravel road that travels south to US Highway 50 near Sargents. About a mile north of the intersection is the road west to Black Sage Pass. The road that continues north from the intersection goes through White Pine, a once thriving mining town, and over Tomichi Pass, Hancock Pass, and Williams Pass. White Pine and the area to the north can also be reached from the Old Monarch Pass road via a Forest Service side road that cuts through No Name Creek.

On the east side of Monarch Pass, at Maysville, a side road up the North Fork of the South Arkansas travels past two Forest Service campgrounds and several lakes; to the north of this road are three 14,000-foot peaks: Mt. Shavano, Mt. Tabeguache, and Mt. Antero. From Garfield, about six miles farther west than Maysville on US Highway 50, another side road follows the Middle Fork of the South Arkansas River toward Chalk Creek Pass and St. Elmo.

The original Monarch Pass route, which is not suitable for passenger cars and is not indicated by any signs, travels to the north of the Old Monarch Pass road, starting on the west at a point several miles below the summit of Old Monarch Pass and on the east by the Monarch ski area about one-half mile below the entrance to the Old Monarch Pass road.

25 Black Sage Pass

Location: between Tomichi Creek near
    Sargents on US Highway 50 and Waunita
    Hot Springs off US Highway 50 near
    Doyleville
Difficulty: can be negotiated by most
    passenger cars under good conditions
Scenic Quality: attractive countryside
Historic Interest: moderate
Side Roads: few in pass vicinity
High Point: 9,745 feet
Maps: USFS map of Gunnison National
    Forest at 1:125,000
USGS sheet 5 of Gunnison County at 1:50,000
Colorado highway map at 1:1,000,000

Black Sage Pass is located along a ridge that separates the upper Tomichi Creek from the equally scenic valley formed by Hot Spring Creek. The Black Sage Pass road dates back to the period around 1880, when unusually rich

veins of silver were discovered near Pitkin. The only direct routes to Pitkin led through the very highest and roughest portions of the Sawatch Range; consequently, the more practical if less direct routes followed Old Monarch Pass or Marshall Pass to Tomichi Creek, then led over the relatively low crossing at Black Sage Pass to Waunita Hot Springs and north to Pitkin. By 1880, wagon trains and daily stages were crossing Black Sage Pass on their way west to Pitkin.

In the summer of 1882, Denver and South Park trains reached Pitkin by way of the spectacular Alpine Tunnel crossing (*see* Williams Pass). But the need for Black Sage Pass continued, since it provided access between Gunnison and the mining town of White Pine (located south of Tomichi Pass), where the population soared to 3,000 during the boom years of the 1880s. In addition, the Black Sage Pass road received the benefit of traffic to and from the early resort town of Waunita Hot Springs, located about four miles west of the summit of Black

The summit of Black Sage Pass.

Sage Pass. Although it was almost invariably the discovery of gold or silver that led to the founding of Colorado's mountain towns, tourism quickly became an important industry at many of the scenic locations throughout the early mining districts. By 1885, Waunita Hot Springs contained a two-story hotel, swimming pools, and bathhouses; the area maintained its status as a resort spa until the turn of the century. Recent studies by the Colorado Geological Survey have shown the geothermal waters at Waunita Hot Springs to be among the hottest in the state.

From the east, Black Sage Pass can be reached either by the Old Monarch Pass road or from a paved road that branches north from US Highway 50 one mile north of Sargents. Both roads lead to the upper end of a lovely farming valley, where a well-marked side road crosses Tomichi Creek and climbs through stands of aspen to a wooded summit that opens onto a spacious and peaceful valley. At an intersection on the floor of the valley, about one-half mile east of Waunita Hot Springs, is the road north over Waunita Pass to Pitkin. The main road continues past Waunita Hot Springs and Hot Springs Reservoir to US Highway 50, about sixteen miles east of Gunnison. For persons traveling to and from the Gunnison area by way of Monarch Pass, the route over Black Sage Pass and Old Monarch Pass is an excellent alternative to the main highway route during the summer and fall, since the distance by back roads is a bit shorter and the extra time required for a leisurely pace through this historic mining area is richly rewarded by the interesting sights and fine scenery.

The east side of Black Sage Pass includes no side roads of particular interest except for the route that continues up Tomichi Creek to Tomichi Pass, Hancock Pass, and the Alpine Tunnel, which are described elsewhere in this section. On the west side of Black Sage Pass are several side roads that travel over a mountain ridge and terminate about two miles east of Pitkin. On the west side of Waunita Hot Springs, several additional back roads wind through the countryside, returning eventually to US Highway 50.

A stand of aspen on the east side of Black Sage pass.

26 Waunita Pass

Location: between Waunita Hot Springs off
   US Highway 50 and Pitkin
Difficulty: can be negotiated by most smaller
   passenger cars under good conditions
Scenic Quality: best scenery on the south
   and nicest views on the north side
Historic Interest: moderate
Side Roads: a few of limited interest
High Point: 10,303 feet
Maps: USFS map of Gunnison National
   Forest at 1:125,000
USGS sheet 5 of Gunnison County at 1:50,000
Colorado highway map at 1:1,000,000

In the 1880s, travelers to the mining town of
Pitkin, located on the banks of Quartz Creek in
eastern Gunnison County, usually approached
the town from the east or the south by way of Old
Monarch Pass and Black Sage Pass or across
Marshall Pass. Both of these routes led to the
early resort town of Waunita Hot Springs, located ten miles south of Pitkin. From Waunita
Hot Springs, the road led up a shallow drainage
to a series of ridges, then down the side of a
mountain to Quartz Creek and the town of Pitkin.

By 1880, when the population of Pitkin had
climbed to more than 1,000, daily stagecoaches
traveled this road over Waunita Pass. Although

A cabin near the site of Bowerman, by the base of Waunita Pass.

Pitkin obtained direct rail service by way of the Alpine Tunnel in 1882, the Waunita Pass road still provided local access to Pitkin and to the resort facilities located at Waunita Hot Springs. Shortly after the turn of the century, an old-time miner, J. C. Bowerman, discovered gold at a site on the south side of Waunita Pass. The ensuing boom, though short-lived, brought in enough population to support a town that included two hotels, five saloons, and five gambling parlors. The town of Bowerman died before the start of World War I and so, too, did the Waunita Pass road cease to exist as a significant route. The Colorado *Year Book* for 1919 does not include Waunita Pass among its listing of the more than sixty passes throughout the state.

The modern Waunita Pass road is a relatively wide and well-graded route through the backcountry between Waunita Hot Springs and Pitkin. Starting one-half mile east of Waunita Hot Springs, the road travels through an attractive and little visited valley, past the town site of Bowerman, then through forests of pine and aspen to the summit of Waunita Pass. From here the road drops more steeply into Pitkin, today a thriving summer resort town. From the south side of the Waunita Pass road, several side roads offer opportunities to explore deeper into Gunnison National Forest. Waunita Pass is also an integral part of the longest and most spectacular backcountry circle pass trip in Colorado that can be negotiated by passenger cars: this day-long route between Gunnison and Chaffee counties makes use of Cottonwood Pass, Cumberland Pass, Waunita Pass, Black Sage Pass, and Old Monarch Pass.

An historic building in Pitkin, by the foot of Waunita Pass.

27 Cumberland Pass

Location: between Pitkin and Tincup
Difficulty: can be negotiated by the majority of passenger cars under good conditions/ caution recommended
Scenic Quality: dramatic summit area with excellent views
Historic Interest: moderate
Side Roads: many of interest
High Point: about 12,020 feet
Maps: USFS map of Gunnison National Forest at 1:125,000
USGS sheet 5 of Gunnison County at 1:50,000
Colorado highway map at 1:1,000,000

The Cumberland Pass road, like so many routes in eastern Gunnison County, was born during that fabulous boom period in the early 1880s when new-found wealth was everywhere and expectations were boundless. In the early days of Tincup, heavy supplies came in over Cottonwood Pass, with its relatively gentle grades, or alternately, supplies and ore traveled by way of the more direct but steeper route over Tincup Pass. Starting in 1882, the Denver, South Park, and Pacific Railroad brought trains through the Alpine Tunnel to Pitkin, located only ten miles south of Tincup.

The two rival towns of Tincup and Pitkin, however, are located in adjacent drainages separated by a long and high ridge running west from the main branch of the Sawatch Range. In 1880, a pack trail was constructed over this ridge at a gap called Cumberland Pass, and two years later the trail was widened to a wagon road over the 12,000-foot-high pass, allowing more or less direct access from Tincup to the Denver, South Park, and Pacific line that passed through Pitkin on its way from the Alpine Tunnel down Quartz Creek to Gunnison. As an added bonus, the Cumberland Pass area itself proved a rich source of

South side view of the Cumberland Pass area.

ore, and several mines of substantial size were sunk into the barren slopes on both sides of the pass summit.

The town of Tincup managed to survive the Panic of 1893, but by World War I the town and the pass road to Pitkin had died. The Colorado *Year Book* for 1919 did not list Tincup among its catalog of Colorado towns and cities, and Cumberland Pass was missing from the state's listing of mountain passes.

The resurrected Cumberland Pass road is the second highest crossing in Colorado that passenger cars can negotiate (Jones Pass is the highest). Due to the long shelf road on the north side of the pass, along with several sharp curves and rough spots, the road should not be traveled by passenger cars with a long wheel base and limited ground clearance. From Tincup, the Cumberland Pass road travels south along an attractive valley through which Willow Creek flows before climbing in a series of switchbacks to the long alpine shelf road that leads to a barren, windswept summit. Directly to the east and north are the high peaks of the Sawatch Range, and to the northwest lies Taylor Park and beyond it the Elk Mountains. From the top of Cumberland Pass, the road drops a bit steeply to the North Fork of Quartz Creek and Pitkin, a twenty-one-mile drive from Tincup. Once in Pitkin, travelers can continue south by back roads over Waunita Pass and Black Sage Pass to the Tomichi Valley or take the paved highway the remainder of the way down Quartz Creek to US Highway 50 and join the highway about ten miles from Gunnison. The road down Quartz Creek deserves special mention as an unusually attractive journey through a quiet ranching area rimmed with interesting rock formations.

The Cumberland Pass area includes an unusual variety of side roads that reach off in nearly every direction. Most of the roads travel to abandoned mining sites, but several eventually return to main roads in the area. In the rugged alpine terrain below the pass summit, but well above timberline, a network of spectacular jeep roads travels to mining sites, mills, and cabins located on both sides of the ridge. Intrepid and well-equipped explorers could easily spend a full day traveling the backcountry roads within a one-half-dozen-mile radius of Cumberland Pass. In addition, three miles above Pitkin is the side road that travels above the Middle Fork of Quartz Creek to the Alpine Tunnel, Williams Pass, Hancock Pass, and Tomichi Pass.

28 Tomichi Pass

Location: between Sargents on US Highway 50
and Brittle Silver Basin
Difficulty: four-wheel-drive required/caution
recommended
Scenic Quality: excellent, with dramatic
summit view and outstanding north side
scenery
Historic Interest: modest
Side Roads: several of special interest
High Point: 11,979 feet
Maps: USFS map of Gunnison National
Forest at 1:125,000
USGS sheet 5 of Gunnison County at 1:50,000

Back in the 1880s, Tomichi Creek, located
just west of the Sawatch Range on the easterly
border of Gunnison County, was teeming with
miners and newly staked claims. White Pine, the
principal settlement, reached a population of
about 3,000, and the population of Tomichi, two
miles to the north, soared at one point to 1,500.
Despite the presence of good-quality ore, access
was a continuing problem. The easiest route in or
out was west over Black Sage Pass to Gunnison
or to Waunita Pass and Pitkin, which was served
by the Denver, South Park, and Pacific railroad.

To the north of White Pine and Tomichi, a
high ridge blocks the way into Brittle Silver
Basin and the gentle grade down Quartz Creek to
Pitkin. The high ridge, however, has a saddle that
dips down to a point just below 12,000 feet, and a
route was soon established over this fearful crossing called Tomichi Pass. The route was not
heavily used even in its heyday, and now it is a
little known but spectacular entrance into and
out of the Brittle Silver Basin.

Starting from the south, the road to Tomichi
Pass begins on US Highway 50 a mile east of Sargents and leads north through a peaceful ranching valley to the town site of White Pine and the

Tomichi Pass from Brittle Silver Basin. Note the shelf road leading to the summit.

former location of Tomichi, which was destroyed by an avalanche that swept through in 1899. Beyond Tomichi, the road becomes rougher and begins climbing steeply in sections as it rises into a long valley that terminates at the pass summit. Spread out below the top of the pass is Brittle Silver Basin, rimmed on the east by the Continental Divide. Across the basin, the Hancock Pass road climbs dramatically up a steep drainage before disappearing over a saddle along the Divide. The summit view is breathtaking and so, too, is the short trip along the north side of Tomichi Pass. Leading down from the summit is a narrow shelf road that descends into the basin and winds roughly over a stream crossing before it travels by the cutoff to Hancock Pass and joins the Quartz Creek road leading west to Pitkin or north to Williams Pass and the Alpine Tunnel. The north side approach to Tomichi Pass from Pitkin is identical to Hancock Pass except that the route continues along the eastern rim of the basin. To reach Tomichi Pass from the north, travel to Pitkin and proceed east from town along the

route to Cumberland Pass and Tincup. About two miles from Pitkin is the road and a route marker to the Alpine Tunnel. Take this road, turning south at a sharp bend about two and one-half miles from the tunnel entrance.

The trip over Tomichi Pass and Hancock Pass, bisecting Brittle Silver Basin, is one of the most rugged and spectacular double pass trips in Colorado. Although the route has probably been successfully negotiated otherwise, it should be attempted only by experienced drivers with narrow-track four-wheel-drive vehicles under good weather conditions.

Most of the side roads and various other pass routes in this portion of eastern Gunnison County are discussed elsewhere in the section. In addition, several interesting side roads exist in the area of White Pine and Tomichi. At Tomichi, rough roads climb up several of the drainages nearly to the top of the Continental Divide. East of White Pine, a network of mining roads leads to the once thriving North Star mine and other sites in the Galena Gulch area.

A reconstructed water tank on the Quartz Creek route to Tomichi and Hancock passes.

29 Hancock Pass

Location: between St. Elmo–Hancock off
US Highway 24 and Pitkin–Gunnison off
US Highway 50
Difficulty: four-wheel-drive strongly recommended on the east side; required on the
west side
Scenic Quality: excellent, with dramatic
summit view
Historic Interest: slight
Side Roads: several of interest
High Point: about 12,140 feet
Maps: USFS map of Gunnison National
Forest at 1:125,000
USFS map of San Isabel National Forest
at 1:125,000
USGS sheet 2 of Chaffee County at 1:50,000
USGS sheet 5 of Gunnison County at 1:50,000

Hancock Pass, a Continental Divide crossing
about one and one-half miles southeast of
Williams Pass, frequently has been confused with
Williams Pass. Indeed, Hancock Pass is sometimes referred to as new Williams Pass. But Hancock is a separate pass route, higher than
Williams Pass, and offers one of the most stunning views anywhere in Colorado. What Hancock
Pass lacks is a documented historical lineage. The
route may long have existed as a trail, but only in
recent years has the pass road connected Hancock and Brittle Silver Basin.

Both the easiest and most scenic direction to
travel Hancock Pass is from the east. Starting on
US Highway 285 south of Buena Vista, the route
goes west on Colorado Highway 162 to Mt.
Princeton Hot Springs and along Chalk Creek,
with Mt. Princeton looming to the north and Mts.
Antero, Shavano, and Tabeguache (all 14,000-

Brittle Silver Basin and Hancock Pass from the top of Tomichi Pass.

foot peaks) to the south. At the old mining town of St. Elmo, the road swings south past Romley, a once thriving community that prospered from the wealth of the Mary Murphy mine, located a mile east of town. Past Romley is the town site of Hancock. Here, the Denver, South Park, and Pacific trains used to begin their steep climb up to the Alpine Tunnel. Just past Hancock and a short distance beyond the side road to the east portal of the Alpine Tunnel and Williams Pass is another side road to the right marked with a small Forest Service sign pointing the way to Hancock Pass. Since Hancock is located above 11,000 feet, the two-mile route to the pass summit quickly emerges from timberline and climbs uneventfully to the top of the pass. At the summit, a spectacular view appears. Beneath a ridge of 13,000-foot peaks rests the Brittle Silver Basin and the headwaters of Quartz Creek; rising above the south side of the basin is a dramatically sculptured saddle with a cliff-hanging shelf road carved into it. This road leads over Tomichi Pass and south to Sargents on US Highway 50, at the base of Monarch and Marshall passes.

From the top of Hancock Pass, a rough and quite steep four-wheel-drive road descends to Brittle Silver Basin. Near Quartz Creek a fork to the left leads along the edge of the basin and over Tomichi Pass. The route to the right joins the main Quartz Creek road about three miles from the west portal of the Alpine Tunnel and about one and one-half miles below the turnoff to Williams Pass from the Alpine Tunnel road. The circle trip over Hancock Pass and Williams Pass, which starts and ends at Hancock, is an excellent though demanding way to view the wildly rugged countryside in the upper reaches of Quartz Creek. From the base of Hancock Pass, alternate exit routes are available either through Pitkin or north over Cumberland Pass and back to the Arkansas Valley by way of Tincup Pass or Cottonwood Pass. To reach Hancock Pass from the west, travel by paved road to Pitkin and proceed north on the route to Cumberland Pass, turning east at the Alpine Tunnel sign. Turn south about two and one-half miles from the tunnel entrance at a sharp bend as the road swings north. Travelers should be aware that the USGS fifteen-minute Garfield quadrangle map of the area ought not be used, since it does not show the west side of the pass road and poorly displays the east side start of the route.

A storefront detail in the town of St. Elmo, on the road to Hancock Pass.

30 Williams Pass and the Alpine Tunnel

Location: between St. Elmo–Hancock and Pitkin–Gunnison

Difficulty: four-wheel-drive required/special difficulties on west side

Scenic Quality: excellent along the entire route

Historic Interest: substantial

Side Roads: several of exceptional scenic and historic interest

High Point: 11,762 feet

Maps: USFS map of Gunnison National Forest at 1:125,000

USFS map of San Isabel National Forest at 1:125,000

USGS sheet 2 of Chaffee County at 1:50,000

USGS sheet 5 of Gunnison County at 1:50,000

The Williams Pass crossing of the Sawatch Range was named for Robert R. Williams, a Denver, South Park, and Pacific engineer who pioneered the wagon road over this high route. Nineteenth-century railroad men normally did not build wagon roads, but the Denver, South Park, and Pacific line was not a typical nineteenth-century railroad, and the pass road served a special purpose. That purpose was a daring construction project known as the Alpine Tunnel, an 1,800-foot-long bore that ranked among the greatest feats of early railroad engineering.

By 1881, John Evans' Denver, South Park, and Pacific line ran up the South Platte Valley, over Kenosha Pass, through South Park, and over Trout Creek Pass to the Arkansas Valley and up the Chalk Creek drainage to the towns of St. Elmo and Hancock. Connecting wagon roads allowed the Denver, South Park, and Pacific to service the Pitkin-Tincup area of eastern Gunnison County by way of Tincup Pass and Williams Pass and to reach the Roaring Fork Valley (Aspen and Ash-

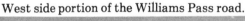
West side portion of the Williams Pass road.

croft) by way of Cottonwood Pass and Taylor Pass. However, Evans was not content with indirect service to the booming Gunnison country that lay west of the Sawatch Range. Beginning in 1880, his work crews began boring a tunnel at an 11,600-foot elevation—a tunnel that would carry Denver and South Park trains from St. Elmo and Hancock to Pitkin and on to Gunnison. Immediately over the tunnel route lay Altman Pass, 12,124 feet high, but the Williams Pass wagon road served to ferry workers and supplies between the two ends of the bore.

For nearly two years, a construction force of 300 to 400 workers labored under conditions of extreme hardship, using sledgehammers and hand-held drills to perforate the rock with blasting holes. The climate and altitude coupled with the isolated location caused enormous turnover; some 10,000 workers served on the project, many lasting only for a day or so. Construction problems abounded. The solid granite exterior had hidden rotten rock, aggregate, and seeping water—an unanticipated problem that reoccurred almost a century later to plague the builders of the Eisenhower Tunnel near Loveland Pass. A half million feet of California redwood had to be imported to reinforce the walls of the Alpine Tunnel, and eight hundred feet of snowsheds were necessary to protect the track from snow accumulation. Some reports state that not a single worker was killed during the construction project.

Despite these heroic efforts, the Alpine Tunnel proved a commercial failure. John Evans' sturdy little narrow gauge locomotives did reach Gunnison, but the Denver and Rio Grande Railway had beaten him there by way of Marshall Pass more than one and one-half years earlier. As on the rail routes over Boreas Pass and Rollins Pass, maintenance costs were extreme, and in 1885 snowstorms kept the tunnel route closed for a number of months. Three years later a cave-in closed the tunnel until 1895, and when a portion of the tunnel collapsed again in 1910, it never reopened. Following the completion of the Alpine Tunnel, the Williams Pass wagon road probably continued to receive some local use, but it was too steep and rough a route to last long.

In fact, the Williams Pass road has barely survived. Contemporary Forest Service and USGS maps still show the pass route, but the Forest Service designates it on its maps as a trail, and no signs indicate its location at either end of the route. In addition, the west side of the pass road is rough and prone to collect standing water, which can turn it into a bottomless quagmire

many hundred yards in length. I have managed to reach the pass summit from the west side, but it required lifting my trails motorcycle out of axle-deep mud at several points. The road is more readily negotiated from east to west so that gravity can favor rather than retard passage along the west side of the route. Regardless of the side of approach, I do not advise driving the road under muddy conditions in a lone motor vehicle. Two or more vehicles should be used to travel the route, and all vehicles should be equipped with winches and high flotation tires.

Despite these problems with mud and with route finding, a trip over Williams Pass is well worth the effort. The countryside on both sides of the pass road is outstanding and of exceptional historic interest. The pass area itself is a seldom visited wonderland of alpine meadows and mountain vistas. In addition, several side roads of special interest are located nearby and travel to the east and west portals of the Alpine Tunnel and to Hancock, Tomichi, and Chalk Creek passes.

From the east, the following route leads to Williams Pass: from US Highway 285 south of Buena Vista, take Colorado Highway 162 west to Mt. Princeton Hot Springs and continue west by dirt road to St. Elmo and south through Romley to the lovely ghost town of Hancock (where passenger cars must stop). A marked side road to the right leads toward the east portal of the Alpine Tunnel, and about one-half mile up this road, another side road branches to the left, climbing steeply to a wooded shelf route that leads directly to the broad meadow below Williams Pass. From the west, travel by paved road to Pitkin and proceed north along the route to Cumberland Pass, turning east at the well-marked route to the Alpine Tunnel. This long and majestic shelf road along the route of the Denver, South Park, and Pacific Railway travels high above Quartz Creek, then swings north past the side road to Hancock Pass and Tomichi Pass and emerges near timberline as an imposing shelf road that terminates dramatically at Alpine Tunnel, the town that once stood by the west portal of John Evans' pet project. About one and one-half miles before Alpine Tunnel, an unmarked side road branches to the right from the tunnel road and begins a rough ascent to the alpine meadow that gives direct access to Williams Pass. The Forest Service 1:125,000 maps accurately portray the west side route but do a less than perfect job of indicating the east side access. The USGS quadrangle sheet (Garfield fifteen-minute quad) is outdated and inaccurate.

31 Tincup Pass

Location: between St. Elmo, off US Highway 24, and Tincup

Difficulty: four-wheel-drive recommended on the east side and required on the west side

Scenic Quality: excellent along the entire route

Historic Interest: moderate

Side Roads: few in the pass vicinity

High Point: 12,154 feet

Maps: USFS map of San Isabel National Forest at 1:125,000

USFS map of Gunnison National Forest at 1:125,000

USGS sheet 2 of Chaffee County at 1:50,000

USGS sheets 3 and 5 of Gunnison County at 1:50,000

View from St. Elmo of the Tincup Pass road.

With the discovery of rich silver deposits in 1879, the area around Tincup quickly boomed; by 1882, Tincup was the largest producer of silver ore in Gunnison County, and the population was reported to be about 6,000. The most direct and earliest route into and out of Tincup Camp led west from the Arkansas River valley to the town of St. Elmo and up the North Fork of Chalk Creek to a high gap in the Continental Divide. This was followed by a rough descent down East Willow Creek to Tincup. The route could not have been easy, but it provided an efficient means of hauling freight into Tincup and taking ore to the smelters located on the east side of the Continental Divide. By 1880, the pass route had been turned into a wagon road with local service provided by Witowski and Dunbar's Hack Line.

As the town of Tincup matured, other routes were used to transport freight and passengers: Cottonwood Pass provided gentle grades for hauling heavy items, and, starting in 1882, Cumberland Pass provided access to Pitkin and the Denver and South Park rail facilities. Down the Taylor River, at Altmont, the Denver and Rio Grande spur line stopped on its way to Crested Butte. But still the rough and scenic Tincup Pass route remained the most direct road to civilization. A map published by the Clason Map Company of Denver in 1919 for the Colorado State Board of Immigration even shows the Tincup Pass route as an automobile road, though it is difficult to believe that many of the early horseless carriages could have struggled over that high ridge—or returned once they reached Tincup.

In many ways, Tincup Camp and Tincup Pass epitomize the early Colorado mining towns and mountain roads. The town, which sits in a high valley surrounded on three sides by mountain ranges well over 12,000 feet high, was once a rough-and-tumble place to reside: during one brief period in the 1880s, three town marshals in a row met untimely fates. The first and third were killed in shoot-outs, and the second died by his own hand. The Tincup Pass road in turn simply travels along the nearest available drainage to timberline and from there marches more or less directly up a scenic alpine meadow to a saddle between two peaks. It then winds along the east side meadow to the nearest creek and travels straight down the valley to St. Elmo. No complex switchbacks, bridges, or other clever artifices used elsewhere by nineteenth-century road builders detract from the simplicity of this route.

From St. Elmo, the pass road begins at the west edge of town at a hand-lettered sign marking the direction to Tincup. In Tincup, the route begins at the crossroads in the center of town. Passenger cars can negotiate the first three miles of the trip from Tincup to lovely Mirror Lake, at the foot of the pass, but from that point the next four miles are four-wheel-drive only. On the east side, from US Highway 285 south of Buena Vista, passenger cars can easily reach St. Elmo by way of Colorado Highway 162 but should not attempt to travel farther west.

The Tincup Pass road itself includes no side roads of note. But on the east side, a road from St. Elmo travels south to Hancock, giving access to Alpine Tunnel, Williams Pass, and Hancock Pass. From Hancock, a deteriorating road leads south toward Chalk Creek Pass and Garfield, near the base of Monarch and Old Monarch Pass. From Tincup, roads lead north to Cottonwood Pass and south to Cumberland Pass and the town of Pitkin. I prefer to start for the Tincup Pass summit from the somewhat more dramatic west side, but travelers who begin at US Highway 285 in the Arkansas Valley can enjoy a leisurely lunch in scenic Tincup and spend the afternoon touring the lovely valleys and high peaks of eastern Gunnison County.

Mirror Lake looking toward Tincup Pass.

32 Cottonwood Pass

Location: between Buena Vista on US
  Highway 24 and Taylor Park–Gunnison
Difficulty: suitable for passenger cars under
  normal conditions
Scenic Quality: very high with excellent
  summit view
Historic Interest: considerable
Side Roads: various of substantial interest
High Point: 12,126 feet
Maps: USFS map of Gunnison National Forest
  at 1:125,000
USFS map of San Isabel National Forest
  at 1:125,000
USGS sheet 3 of Gunnison County at 1:50,000
USGS sheet 2 of Chaffee County at 1:50,000
Colorado highway map at 1:1,000,000

The upper valley of the Arkansas River is separated from Gunnison County by the Sawatch Range, a magnificent and forbidding line of mountains that dominates the western skyline of the valley. For centuries, a thin route of trails linked the valley with the high, broad expanse of Taylor Park. But the impetus for the construc-

tion of pass roads along the eastern border of Gunnison County came shortly after gold was discovered in the Leadville area.

By 1879, the population of Leadville had swelled to more than 5,000; the town included a hotel with 151 rooms; 17 smelters; and 30 sawmills. The rush was on to discover another bonanza of like proportions. Impressive pots of gold did indeed lie over the hills. Rich ore deposits were soon discovered in Tincup, Pitkin, the Ashcroft area near Aspen, and other less well-remembered locations. Cottonwood Pass was nicely situated to serve these areas. From Buena Vista and direct rail access along the Arkansas Valley, the pass route led through the Collegiate Group (a part of the Sawatch Range) between Mt. Yale and Mt. Princeton, over the Continental Divide, and into Taylor Park. To the southwest lay Gunnison and the San Juans; to the northwest over Taylor Pass was Ashcroft, Ute City (Aspen), and the Roaring Fork Valley; to the south of the pass a route led to Tincup. By 1880, an improved road had been constructed over Cottonwood Pass. Until Independence Pass was opened in November 1881, Cottonwood Pass served as the main supply route into the Roaring Fork Valley from

The Cottonwood Pass road emerging from timberline. Mt. Princeton rises to the right. Note a stretch of older road bisecting the modern route on the left.

The Collegiate Group and winding roadway on the west side of Cottonwood Pass. *Courtesy, Dick Hart.*

Leadville and Buena Vista. Even afterward it remained an important route into Tincup, Taylor Park, and various points beyond.

As a commercial venture, however, the Cottonwood Pass toll road soon failed. Marshall Sprague reports in *The Great Gates* that in 1882 the toll road reverted to Chaffee County ownership. It had become still another financial casualty of the boom-and-bust economy that accompanied the western mining rushes. Happily, the Cottonwood Pass route was not to suffer the same fate as many other roads spawned by the search for gold and silver. In 1960, the Forest Service reconstructed the route and it opened once again to travelers over the Collegiate Range. The motivation for reopening the road was more practical than nostalgic. Cottonwood Pass not only provides direct access from the east to Taylor Park Reservoir, it remains the most direct route from the upper Arkansas Valley into Gunnison and Montrose.

The reconstructed Cottonwood Pass road is wide, well graded, and well marked. Under good weather conditions, the only hazard is dust, which billows up from the road in rolling white clouds during periods of heavy summertime traffic. This nuisance notwithstanding, the trip over Cottonwood Pass is a memorable experience. From both sides, the road winds gently upward through forests of pine and fir to an alpine summit yielding a marvelous panoramic view. A hike above the summit affords an even better view of the surrounding countryside.

As an additional bonus, the Cottonwood Pass area is laced with scenic and interesting side roads. On the east side of the pass are several worthwhile roads to abandoned mining sites, and on the west side, an extensive network of roads branches off to the north and the south. At the east end of Taylor Park Reservoir is the road south along Willow Creek to Tincup and Tincup Pass, Cumberland Pass, and Hancock Pass. At the northeast corner of the reservoir, a graded road travels up the Taylor River, and a four-wheel-drive route goes over Taylor Pass to Aspen. From each of these routes and elsewhere along the main road through Taylor Park, side roads branch out along the drainage ways.

To reach Cottonwood Pass from the Gunnison area, take State Highway 135 north from Gunnison about ten miles to the town of Almont, travel northeast to the reservoir, and at the northeast corner of the reservoir, take the main road east. From the Arkansas Valley, Cottonwood Pass is reached by way of State Highway 306, which travels west up Cottonwood Creek from the intersection with US Highway 24 in downtown Buena Vista.

33 Hagerman Pass

Location: between Leadville on US Highway 24 and Basalt on Colorado Highway 82
Difficulty: four-wheel-drive needed for west side summit stretch/most passenger cars can negotiate lower portions of the road
Scenic Quality: excellent near summit and on the west side
Historic Interest: high
Side Roads: many of interest on the west side
High Point: **11,925 feet**
Maps: USFS map of White River National Forest at 1:125,000
USGS single sheet of Lake County at 1:50,000
USGS sheet 2 of Pitkin County at 1:50,000

From the top of Mosquito Pass, high above Leadville, the Sawatch Range reaches out across the horizon, a snowcapped jumble of peaks and gaps. The gap directly west from Mosquito Pass, sixteen miles distant, is Hagerman Pass, a high Continental Divide crossing with a history as complex and bizarre as any pass route in Colorado.

James J. Hagerman was a Milwaukee banker who brought considerable wealth and an advanced case of tuberculosis with him to Colorado. For entertainment in his declining years, Hagerman bought mining properties in Leadville and Aspen and later Cripple Creek. These mines yielded him more millions of dollars. Some say out of sheer perversity, he and a group of Colorado Springs businessmen decided to build a railroad that would compete with the Denver and Rio Grande. It was not to be the usual narrow gauge line but a standard gauge railroad between Colorado Springs and Aspen. In short order, Hagerman raised some $7 million, and his Colorado Midland Railway Company began laying tracks toward Leadville. Once in Leadville, the Colorado

A view of Ivanhoe Lake and the upper Fryingpan Valley from near the summit of Hagerman Pass.

Midland route turned west toward Busk Creek and a crossing too high for any railroad to reach.

Like the Denver and South Park at Altman Pass, Colorado Midland work crews began blasting a tunnel through more than one-fifth mile of rock at an 11,500-foot elevation. The Colorado Midland was more fortunate than the Denver, South Park and Pacific, which had encountered rotten rock and seeping water at the Alpine Tunnel, and in 1886 Hagerman's tunnel was finished. Two years and several legal battles later, the Colorado Midland was in Aspen, competing with the Denver and Rio Grande for the lucrative revenues that could be collected from hauling ore out of the Roaring Fork Valley. Having made his point, Hagerman sold the Colorado Midland at a profit to the Santa Fe line, an archrival of the Denver and Rio Grande, and turned his attention to making money elsewhere in Colorado. It was a wise move.

The problems of snow accumulation and avalanches that plagued the Alpine Tunnel also caused high maintenance costs and lost revenues at the Hagerman Tunnel. Consequently, a second tunnel was completed at the 10,700-foot level in 1893. This bore, nearly five times longer than the original tunnel, was constructed at a cost of $3 million by a private company hoping to profit from the need for a lower crossing. The venture did indeed make money, but even the new Busk–Ivanhoe Tunnel failed to survive. The line was bought during World War I by another mining baron, Albert Carlton, who renamed the lower tunnel in his own honor and converted it into an automobile tunnel from 1924 to 1937. In the 1960s, Charlie Boustead, a colorful figure in his own right, and various eastern slope water users convinced the U.S. Congress to fund a vast transmountain diversion project known as the Fryingpan–Arkansas. To facilitate the diversion of western slope water into Turquoise Reservoir, near Leadville, the Corps of Engineers constructed still another tunnel below Hagerman Pass—the four-mile-long Charles H. Boustead Tunnel.

While this confusing passage of events was occurring below the surface of the Sawatch Range, activity also was taking place above it at Hagerman Pass. The original trail crossing never received heavy traffic until a road was developed principally to move men and equipment between either side of the original tunnel during construction. For a number of years, the route fell into disrepair, but it served again for the construction of the Fryingpan–Arkansas project and for the building of a Denver to Grand Junction high-voltage transmission line.

To reach Hagerman Pass from the east, follow the signs to Turquoise Reservoir from US Highway 24 at Leadville, and three and one-half miles west of the dam take an unmarked side road to the left. The road gently climbs Busk Creek and turns 180 degrees at the entrance to the Carlton (Busk–Ivanhoe) Tunnel, ascending the other side of the creek and climbing through a high pine forest that opens onto an impressive view of the **Arkansas Valley, Leadville, and the Mosquito Range. By a Forest Service signboard describing the history of the Colorado Midland Railway a wide hiking trail follows the old railroad grade to the Hagerman Tunnel entrance. Beyond this point the road becomes rougher and passes along a narrow divide perched dramatically above Hagerman Lake, then tops a wide, nearly flat summit before starting a steep and somewhat rough descent to Ivanhoe Lake and the Fryingpan River. The descending west side view is marvelous. After leveling off, the road passes by Hell Gate, a scenic spot where the railroad used to stop so that passengers could marvel at the countryside. The long descent along the Fryingpan continues past Nast, a major stop on the Colorado Midland route, and travels by several more late nineteenth-century town sites and the lovely Ruedi Reservoir before finally exiting on Colorado Highway 82 at Basalt.

Except for the circular drive around Turquoise Lake and several spur roads, there are few byways of interest on the east side of Hagerman Pass. But the west side of the pass more than compensates for this lack. Near Nast and Hell Gate are side roads that wind along Ivanhoe Creek and the Fryingpan River, passing near the entrance to the various tunnels on the west side. At Biglow, Thomasville, and Norris, additional side roads travel up a variety of local drainages into the backcountry of the White River National Forest. To take one example, the road north from Thomasville follows a circuitous route over Crooked Creek Pass (see No. 58, Crooked Creek Pass) to West Brush Creek, exiting on a long but good road to the town of Eagle on Interstate 70. The summit stretch and west side of the Hagerman Pass road certainly rank among the nicer routes in Colorado, but no trip through the area is complete without sufficient time to explore deeper into the Fryingpan River basin.**

34 Pearl Pass

Location: between Crested Butte on Colorado Highway 135 and Aspen on Colorado Highway 82

Difficulty: four-wheel-drive required/special caution mandatory

Scenic Quality: outstanding along the entire route

Historic Interest: considerable

Side Roads: several of special interest

High Point: 12,705 feet

Maps: USFS map of Gunnison National Forest at 1:125,000

USFS map of White River National Forest at 1:125,000

USGS sheets 2 and 3 of Gunnison County at 1:50,000

USGS sheets 1 and 2 of Pitkin County at 1:50,000

The Pearl Pass road has a well-deserved reputation as the most rugged and difficult pass road in the Elk Range and, perhaps, anywhere in Colorado. It is steep, narrow, often snow-blocked, prone to mud, littered with loose rock, long, exposed, and exhausting to travel even under good conditions. Why would anyone bother to use a road like this? The answer is quite simple. Pearl Pass is an historic crossing between two of Colorado's most fabled mining towns turned into internationally known recreation areas. At lower elevations, the pass road travels through consistently beautiful countryside that becomes wildly spectacular as the route traverses miles of remote alpine terrain. Due to fortunate accidents of geology and geography, the Elk Range offers a unique combination of lush, gaily flowered meadows topped by peaks and ridge walls layered in rich colors.

Of course, the Pearl Pass road was not built for the purpose of providing access to this alpine wonderland. Instead, its history is tied to the accomplishments of the Denver and Rio Grande Railway. The 1880s were the heyday of Colorado's adventuresome narrow gauge railroads, and the D&RG was no exception. In 1881, General Palmer's work crews had pushed tracks over Cumbres Pass en route to the San Juan mining camps and taken the Gunnison branch of the D&RG north from the town of Gunnison to Crested Butte. Not only did the Denver and Rio Grande beat its rival line, the Denver and South Park, to Gunnison by more than a year, but it could profit from the rich bituminous and anthracite coal mines developing around Crested Butte.

In addition, Crested Butte was only two

Elk Range scene from the Pearl Pass road.

dozen miles away from Ashcroft and thirty-five miles from Aspen, where a silver boom of immense proportions was underway despite the lack of a handy route into the upper reaches of the Roaring Fork Valley. To bring Crested Butte and Aspen closer, a rough wagon road was constructed up the Middle Fork of Brush Creek to a very high crossing and then down the even steeper north side of the Elks to Castle Creek. The wagon road was among the worst in the Colorado Rockies—so bad, in fact, that for a time stagecoach drivers reportedly had to disassemble their rigs and winch them along stretches of the route. Despite the opening of a road over Independence Pass shortly before the Pearl Pass road had been completed, Pearl Pass continued to carry a substantial volume of traffic for several years. By 1887, however, the Denver and Rio Grande reached Aspen, and a year later, J. J. Hagerman's Colorado Midland Railway was there, too, eliminating almost entirely the need to use that awful wagon road.

Today, traffic on the Pearl Pass road is composed of recreational users along with an occasional rancher or Forest Service employee. Because the road is poorly marked and usually snow-blocked until late in the season, and also perhaps because of its reputation, the Pearl Pass road is lightly used on both sides of the summit. Travelers intending to cross the road should inquire locally to determine if the summit portion is open in order to avoid a needless traverse of the long shelf roads that lead to the top from both sides.

To reach Pearl Pass from the south, take the Brush Creek road from Colorado Highway 135 about two miles south of Crested Butte. After five miles of travel through private ranching country, the road climbs and winds through lush valleys where cattle graze amid the wild flowers and the brightly sculptured walls of the Elk Range loom increasingly near. Near timberline, the road begins to ascend in several severe pitches, emerging onto a double-tiered set of mead-

South side shelf road leading to the top of Pearl Pass. Snow still blocked motor vehicle travel in late August.

ows that lead to a high, narrow, and not very secure shelf road that tops the pass. It descends in the same spectacular fashion through an eerie basin strewn with fallen boulders and loose rock. Another narrow, off-camber stretch of road leads down to more alpine meadows and a very steep, rather rough descent to Castle Creek. From Castle Creek, the road travels more gently through a lovely forest, ending about one and one-half miles south of Ashcroft and about a dozen miles from Colorado Highway 82 on the west side of Aspen. The north side of the Pearl Pass road affords an exceptional view of the stunning ridge that forms the eastern boundary of the Maroon Bells–Snowmass Wilderness area. This beautifully colored wall begins on the north at Hayden Peak (named for the surveyor, unlike Hayden Pass) and continues to Cathedral Peak and Conundrum Peak. It ends with 14,265-foot-high Castle Peak, which can also be glimpsed from the south side of Pearl Pass.

Both from the standpoint of scenic value and difficulty, the two sides of Pearl Pass are about equal. The principal difference lies in the length of the route, which is about five miles on the north side and about sixteen miles from the highway on the south side. The south side approach is more remote and also more likely to present problems with mud and swollen stream crossings, but the north side accumulations of snow tend to linger through the summer. My personal preference is for the south side approach, time permitting.

The south side of Pearl Pass also offers a wider selection of side roads. From the pass road up Middle Brush Creek, side roads branch up West and East Brush creeks. The Cement Creek road, which starts on Colorado Highway 135 about four miles south of the Brush Creek road, travels past Italian Mountain, a striking peak that was known to members of the Hayden Survey, and on to several abandoned mining sites located high in the Elks.

On the north side of Pearl Pass is the road up Express Creek to Taylor Pass; there is also the unpaved upper portion of the Castle Creek road, which ends at the southern flank of Taylor Peak. Only one side road branches off from the north side of the route to Pearl Pass, but this back road deserves special mention. Starting at the 11,000-foot level, at the point where the Pearl Pass road begins to deteriorate, the road climbs spectacularly to the Montezuma mine, where rich silver deposits were discovered in 1882. The mere sight of this road from below is sufficient to strike fear in the heart of a flatlander, but in fact it is more easily negotiated than the upper portion of the Pearl Pass road, and it affords a stunning view of Castle and Conundrum peaks.

To the northwest of Pearl Pass, along the border and the interior of the Maroon Bells–Snowmass Wilderness area, is an extensive network of 12,000- to 13,000-foot trails over crossings such as Electric Pass, Triangle Pass, Copper Pass, and the Maroon Passes East and West. Travelers attempting these long and demanding but spectacular hiking trails should consult recognized source of route information before setting out.

35 Taylor Pass

Location: between Taylor Park and Aspen
Difficulty: four-wheel-drive required
Scenic Quality: exceptionally good with outstanding summit views
Historic Interest: considerable
Side Roads: several of high scenic value
High Point: 11,928 feet
Maps: USFS map of Gunnison National Forest
    at 1:125,000
USFS map of White River National Forest
    at 1:125,000
USGS sheet 3 of Gunnison County at 1:50,000
USGS sheet 2 of Pitkin County at 1:50,000

In many respects, the Taylor Pass road is a practical man's Pearl Pass. Taylor Pass is neither quite as high, rough or spectacular as its westerly neighbor and one-time rival for the traffic to the Aspen area. Yet it is a lovely route over a de-

manding road that travels through some of the nicest countryside in Colorado accessible to a motor vehicle.

The history of the Taylor Pass road slightly predates but is otherwise similar to that of the road over Pearl Pass. By 1880, it was becoming clear to almost everyone concerned—miners, merchants, financiers, and the displaced Utes—that the silver deposits in the upper Roaring Fork Valley could make Aspen into the second Leadville. That prospect would hardly fill the hearts of present-day Aspen residents with joy, but it excited those early prospectors who had risked the vengeance of the Utes and braved a harsh environment in search of rich, ore-bearing veins that would rival the fabulous mines above Leadville.

The problem with the Roaring Fork Valley was and still remains one of access: how to get supplies in and ore out. In 1880, local business interests organized the Twin Lakes and Roaring Fork Toll Company to construct a road over the

Taylor Lake and the Sawatch Range from Taylor Pass summit.

high crossing then called Hunter's Pass and known now as Independence Pass. But, in the meantime, a good wagon road over Cottonwood Pass connected Buena Vista and Taylor Park, to the south of Aspen. The Denver and Rio Grande and the Denver and South Park railroads were rapidly laying down track in the direction of Buena Vista and Leadville. From the Cottonwood Pass route, a connecting spur road was readily constructed along the flat expanse of Taylor Park, following the Taylor River to its headwaters and crossing over a gap in the Elk Range only six miles from Ashcroft and the gentle grade down Castle Creek to Aspen. The trip from Buena Vista to Aspen over two 12,000-foot passes was not an easy route for man or beast. But the road was in use by 1879 and continued to carry traffic even after the Independence Pass road opened in the winter of 1881 and the Pearl Pass road came into existence the following year.

Eventually, Independence Pass became the preferred route into Aspen, since it provided a more direct linkage with Leadville. By 1888, both the Denver and Rio Grande and the Colorado Midland had reached Aspen, further diminishing the need for Taylor Pass, even though the route was also used for stagecoach service between St. Elmo and Aspen. A decade or so ago, the Taylor Pass road had a reputation as one of the very roughest jeep trips in the Colorado Rockies, but improvements to the south side of the road have brought it to the point where do-it-yourself road building is not normally required to make the trip.

Starting at the north end of Taylor Reservoir, which can be reached either from Gunnison or by way of Cottonwood Pass from Buena Vista, the route follows the broad expanse of Taylor Park up the Taylor River to the abandoned town sites of Dorchester and Bowman. Both were mining towns, and Bowman was also a stage stop and shipping point on the Taylor Pass road. About two miles beyond the Dorchester Campground, a Forest Service sign marks the right-hand fork leading to Taylor Pass, which is about five miles away. The pass road begins climbing in a heavily wooded area, then enters a very rough streambed that can be filled with treacherously deep water. After emerging from the stream about 150 feet later, the road climbs through forested lands to timberline, where it begins ascending more steeply to the edge of Taylor Lake, situated in a lovely basin at the bottom of the imposing headwall crossed by Taylor Pass. Three roads connect the lake and pass summit. The road traveling north around Taylor Lake diverges into a precipitously steep, direct climb, which should not be taken, and a switchbacked route that allows a much safer ascent of the headwall. A third and more scenic road winds west around the lake, climbing very steeply for a short distance before it traverses two smaller alpine lakes and gently climbs in an arc to the top of Taylor Pass. From this scenic summit ridge overlooking Taylor Park and the Sawatch Range, the pass road descends into a rocky gulch that leads to Express Creek and a narrow, occasionally bumpy descent of about three and one-half miles to the Castle Creek road a short distance north of Ashcroft. Travelers approaching the pass from Aspen and Colorado Highway 82 will find the route indicated by a small sign on the Castle Creek road.

The Taylor Pass area offers a variety of interesting side trips. On the east side of the pass, about one mile before the Dorchester Campground, a side road winds up Tellurium Creek toward Ptarmigan Lake and toward a trail route crossing of the Elks that leads west to the Taylor Pass road and north into the Lincoln Creek area below Independence Pass. At the summit of Taylor Pass, side roads diverge to the west and to the east; both routes afford a stunning view of the surrounding countryside. Less than one mile north of the Taylor Pass summit, at the switchback leading into Express Creek, an unmarked side road to the west climbs back up to the ridge, then leads south through a vast expanse of alpine terrain around McArthur Mountain. Travelers can either descend along Queens Gulch to the Castle Creek road or continue by this back route into Aspen.

36 Schofield Pass

Location: between Crested Butte on Colorado
Highway 135 and Marble near Colorado
Highway 133
Difficulty: four-wheel-drive required for west
side of pass/caution advised
Scenic Quality: beautiful countryside with
spectacular scenery along the Crystal River
Historic Interest: moderate
Side Roads: several of high scenic value
High Point: 10,707 feet
Maps: USFS map of Gunnison National
Forest at 1:125,000
USGS sheet 1 of Gunnison County at 1:50,000
USGS sheet 1 of Pitkin County at 1:50,000
Colorado highway map at 1:1,000,000

The famous powerhouse on the Crystal River above
Marble. *Courtesy, State of Colorado.*

Between the East River and the headwaters
of the Crystal River is a relatively low and gentle
ridge that existed as a crossing for centuries. In
the middle of the 1870s, a team from the Hayden
Survey crossed this ridge at Schofield Pass while
exploring the area. The 1877 *Atlas of Colorado*
duly reflected their findings: a secondary road extended north from Crested Butte to the site of
Gothic, and from there a trail continued over the
pass and down what was then called Rock Creek
to its confluence with the Roaring Fork a short
distance from the Colorado River.

Prospectors had found evidence of gold and
silver on both sides of Schofield Pass well before
the Hayden men visited the area, but it was not
until the period around 1880 that major strikes
occurred. The quality of the ore throughout the
region was very good, sometimes averaging as
much as $10,000 to $15,000 per ton. Cities sprang
up at Gothic (where the population soared temporarily to 8,000), Schofield, Crystal, and Marble.
The Schofield Pass route developed into a wagon
road with stage service from Crested Butte to
Crystal. The fame of the area was sufficient that
General U.S. Grant, accompanied by ex-
Governor Routt, visited the towns along the
Schofield Pass road in 1880.

In the years following the Panic of 1893, the
entire area between Crested Butte and Marble fell
into decline, though the famous marble quarries
continued to operate until 1941. The quality of
stone located along Yule Creek is among the
highest-grade quarrying marble in the world, and
the town of Marble once boasted an enormous
marble finishing plant operated by the Colorado
Yule Marble Company. But high transportation
costs and declining demand finally caused the
quarries to close. Natural hazards also were a

chronic problem. The Crystal River valley is
prone to avalanches and mud slides. A massive
mud slide destroyed much of Marble in 1941, and
the Schofield Pass road is periodically blocked by
winter and spring avalanches that keep the road
closed into late August.

In recent years, however, the popularity of
the Schofield Pass area has climbed dramatically.
A proposed downhill ski site near Marble did not
materialize (due to slope instability problems),
but the development of a major ski resort at
Crested Butte and the growth in tourism has
brought newfound popularity to the area on both
sides of Schofield Pass. The reason for this re-
newed interest is not difficult to understand.
Even Colorado natives accustomed to the beauty
of the Rockies long remember a visit to Gothic,
Emerald Lake, and the Crystal River canyon.
Residents of Marble say that when the Ute Indians were driven out of the area, they placed a
curse upon it. Anyone who has visited the majestic Crystal River valley call well appreciate the
Utes' sentiments.

To reach Schofield Pass from the west, take
Colorado Highway 133 to the east base of Mc-
Clure Pass, where a well-maintained side road
travels up the Crystal River valley to the town of

The Schofield Pass road as it begins its descent into the Crystal River canyon.

Marble. Beyond Marble, where passenger cars should stop, the road climbs along a spectacular and notorious shelf route to the site of Crystal. In the spring, awesome volumes of water cascade down the verdant canyon walls in a majestic display of natural forces that have cut deep fissures in the near vertical face of the walls. From Crystal, the road travels through the Devil's Punch Bowl, alongside a marvelous waterfall, and up the very steep, rough grade of the Crystal Canyon to Schofield Park. It then makes a short climb to the wooded pass summit. The descent route is more gentle, dropping past magnificent Emerald Lake onto a lovely subalpine meadow, then down to the splendid valley where Gothic is located. From Gothic, an improved gravel road winds around Snodgrass Mountain and past the instant-chalet architecture of Mt. Crested Butte to the town of Crested Butte, on Colorado Highway 135. To reach Schofield Pass from the east, take Colorado Highway 135 to Crested Butte and continue to the north, following the signs to Mt. Crested Butte and Gothic.

Most smaller, agile passenger cars can readily travel the route from Crested Butte to the top of Schofield Pass. Stories abound of passenger cars that have completed the entire trip. But I doubt that it has happened often and cannot recommend trying it under any conditions. Schofield Pass is a low and gentle crossing, but the canyon and shelf road require caution and the proper motor vehicle for a safe journey. Drivers who are tempted to ignore this advice or risk the curse of the Utes should bear in mind that the Schofield Pass road was the site of the worst Colorado backcountry vehicle accident in recent times, which occurred when an entire carload of sightseers fell to their death.

No trip to Schofield Pass is complete without an opportunity to travel the extensive network of side roads and hiking trails in the area. On the East River side of the pass, at Gothic, a four-wheel-drive route ascends Copper Creek to a lake high in the Elk Range. From there, hiking trails lead over East Maroon Pass and Copper Pass into the Maroon Bells-Snowmass Wilderness. The East Maroon Pass route was used as a wagon crossing between Gothic and Aspen in the 1880s but is now partly within the Maroon Bells-Snowmass Wilderness area. About two miles beyond Gothic, a side road travels up Rustler Gulch to several mining sites. Just north of the pass summit, an unmarked road to the west leads to an alternate crossing known locally as Paradise Divide. The Paradise Divide road travels past the Paradise mine and after crossing the ridge it drops down to Pittsburg, where one of the richest silver mines in Colorado was located. From Pittsburg, other side roads lead up Poverty Gulch to Angel Pass and Daisey Pass, at the north end of the Ruby Range. Several miles below Pittsburg, on the Slate River road to Crested Butte, a side

road travels up picturesquely named Oh-be-Joyful Creek into the Ruby Range, and a hiking trail continues past the road's end to Oh-be-Joyful Pass.

On the Crystal River side of Schofield Pass, near Marble, a magnificent and lightly traveled side road climbs up to the Lead King mine site and Lead King Basin, on the west side of Snowmass Mountain, before descending a rough but beautifully forested route to the pass road. At Marble, a side road to the north leads into the proposed ski area, and another side road of considerable historic interest travels along Yule Creek, past the site of the vast marble quarries, to a trail head and hiking routes that lead over Anthracite Pass and Yule Pass. The Yule Creek wagon road, constructed in 1905, saw heavy service by freight wagons that hauled out the blocks of stone for cutting and for rail shipment from Marble.

View of Mt. Crested Butte, center background, from the Schofield Pass road.

37, 38 Ohio and Kebler Passes

Location: between Gunnison and the North
  Fork Valley
Difficulty: suitable for most passenger cars
  under normal conditions
Scenic Quality: very attractive area; especially
  nice on the south side of Ohio Pass
Historic Interest: modest
Side Roads: many available in the area
High Points: 10,033 feet (Ohio Pass) and
  10,000 feet (Kebler Pass)
Maps: USFS map of Gunnison National
  Forest at 1:125,000
USGS sheets 2 and 4 of Gunnison County
  at 1:50,000
Colorado highway map at 1:1,000,000

These two low but scenic passes in north-western Gunnison County provide a convenient crossing at a low point between the Ruby Range and the Anthracite Range, which are offshoots of the West Elk Mountains. Ohio and Kebler passes, which are separated by less than two miles, form a link between the main branch and the North Fork of the Gunnison River. The two pass roads also yield backcountry travelers access to many hundred square miles of nicely forested countryside in the vicinity of the West Elks.

The Ohio and Kebler Pass routes were once part of an extensive Ute Indian trail system stretching the length of the Colorado Rockies and into northeastern Utah. Following the discovery of gold near the summit of Kebler Pass, a road was constructed over Ohio Pass for freight hauling and stagecoach travel from Gunnison. Coal mining east of Kebler Pass, at the Floresta mine to the west of Ohio Pass, and also along the route from Gunnison to Ohio Pass, led to further development in the area. The Denver and Rio Grande rail lines once ran from Gunnison to the Ohio Pass area and from Crested Butte close to the summit of Kebler Pass.

Just east of the Kebler Pass summit is the

Intersection of the Ohio and Kebler pass roads. *Courtesy, Dick Hart.*

88

THE BRIGHT PROMISE OF
RUBY SILVER, DREW 5,000
PEOPLE TO THIS AREA IN
1879, FROM AS FAR AS
ENGLAND AND SCOTLAND.
IRWIN BECAME A GHOST
TOWN WHEN SILVER WAS
DEMONETIZED IN 1884.
THIS CEMETERY WAS
KNOWN AS RUBY CAMP
CEMETERY IN 1879.
IT WAS RENAMED IRWIN
CEMETERY IN 1880.
APPROXIMATELY 50
BURIALS WERE MADE
HERE BEFORE IT WAS
ABANDONED IN 1885.

Commemorative marker by the summit of Kebler Pass. *Courtesy, Dick Hart.*

old Irwin cemetery, where about fifty persons are interred. A plaque and headstone mark the site beside the road. A bit farther east of the cemetery is a road network leading north into the Irwin town site, Lake Irwin, and numerous abandoned mining operations. These ruins mark the site of a short-lived silver rush, from 1879 to 1885, that saw the rise and fall of two towns and several mining camps in the area. Irwin, the largest of the communities, thrived for a brief time. Perry Eberhart, in his *Guide to the Colorado Ghost Towns and Mining Camps*, reports that the main street of Irwin was a mile long and that nearly two dozen saloons, along with an ample supply of gambling

dens and "parlor houses," once flourished there. Former President U. S. Grant visited Irwin on his trip around the world, and the town was also visited by a recent Harvard graduate named Teddy Roosevelt. Wild Bill Hickok is said to have spent some time in Irwin, but reports of his visit are surely exaggerated, since he was murdered in Deadwood, Dakota Territory, three years before the town site was founded.

To reach Ohio and Kebler passes from the south, take State Highway 135 about three miles north from Gunnison and turn left up Ohio Creek on a well-paved road. This road slowly climbs through a magnificent and unspoiled valley with an excellent view of the West Elk Mountains. At the right times of the year, a dazzling carpet of wild flowers spreads out along the valley floor and hillsides. After the road ascends from the valley, it winds upward through a lovely forest, thick with stands of enormous aspen. About one mile short of the rounded Ohio Pass summit is a side road to the west leading to Lily Lake and the mining site of Floresta. About two miles beyond the summit of Ohio Pass is an intersection. To the right lies a spur road down Coal Creek to Crested Butte, and to the left the main road continues over Kebler Pass and down a wide, smoothly graded route along Anthracite Creek to State Highway 133, by Paonia Reservoir. West from Paonia Reservoir is a circular route along four more reservoirs on the return trip to Gunnison. The route east from Paonia Reservoir leads over McClure Pass and north to Glenwood Springs or south by way of Schofield Pass to Crested Butte and Gunnison.

A variety of side roads, mostly of short length, can be found on both sides of the two passes. In addition, the area is crosscut by an extensive network of hiking trails that lead principally into the Ruby Range north of Irwin and into the West Elk Wilderness by way of Beckwith Pass and Swampy Pass.

The Capital City way station on the road to Engineer Pass. *Courtesy, Dick Hart.*

San Juan Passes: 39 – 50

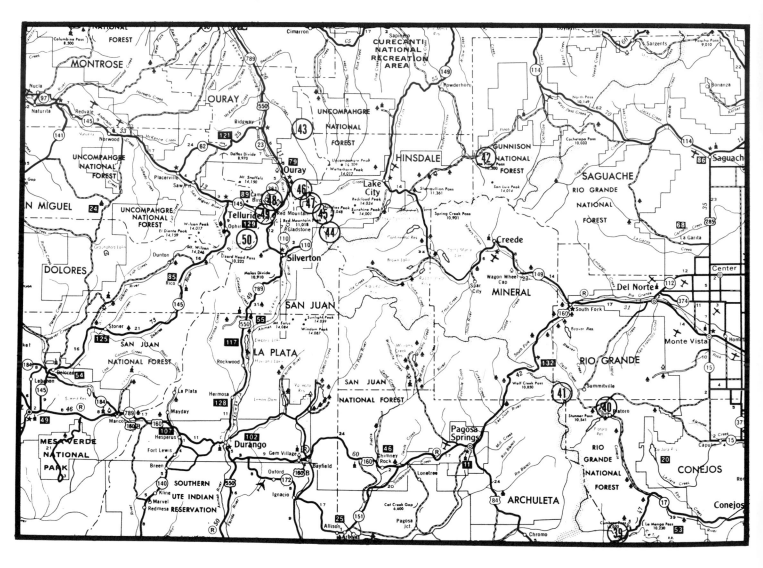

Part Five
San Juan Passes

The San Juan country is an immense mountainscape of some ten thousand square miles—larger than the commonwealth of Massachusetts—covered by massive peaks, splendid valleys, high meadows, and fast-moving streams. The San Juans are not a single set of peaks and ridges but a convoluted series of mountain ranges that includes two main branches of the San Juans, the San Miguel Mountains, the Sneffels Range, the Needle Mountains, and several lesser groups.

San Juan country is a very special place for a number of reasons. First, the San Juans are a geologically complex formation created by the sculpting effect of wind, water, and glaciers on earlier volcanic upheavals. Second, the Continental Divide winds along the eastern edge of the area, creating a convoluted pattern of basins and panoramic mountain vistas. The result is a visual effect quite different from the look of the front range or the Sangre de Cristos. Third, the lush vegetation and red-orange rock formations combine to create scenes more colorful than those found anywhere else in the Colorado Rockies except for in the Elks. Then, too, the legacy of nineteenth-century settlement in the San Juans is still very much in evidence, giving visitors and residents alike a strong sense of historical continuity and cultural heritage.

Once the heartland of the Ute Indians, the San Juans were among the later mountain regions of Colorado to be overrun by settlers in search of wealth. The Utes were long able to keep legal control of their homeland, until their birthright was forever diminished by the Brunot Treaty of 1873. Additionally, the San Juans were sufficiently remote from population centers and so well guarded by huge walls of rock that few bothered, or dared, to venture within. Back in 1860, Charles Baker led a small band of explorers over Cinnamon Pass and into the Animas Valley at a spot just north of present-day Silverton. In the following year, he returned with a larger group of settlers, intending to stake out a mineral-rich territory for the benefit of Southern sympathizers. But the Civil War brought his efforts to an abrupt conclusion. The assault on the San Juans would wait for nearly another one and one-half decades.

When the assault did happen in the mid 1870s, it came with a vengeance. Miners, merchants, jackwackers, wagon masters, engineers, surveyors, geologists, gamblers, prostitutes, and every other manner of humanity poured into the San Juans from the north, the east, and the south. They traveled up the Uncompahgre River to Ouray, established at the head of an awesome box canyon. They came over Cinnamon Pass and Stony Pass to the upper reaches of the Animas River, cradled in the heartland of the San Juans. They wandered up the San Miguel River to Telluride, established at the end of an even more majestic canyon. And they traveled north from Durango along the Animas River to Silverton, once a town so lawless and violent that the town fathers imported Bat Masterson from Dodge City to bring a semblance of proper frontier order.

The men of the San Juan Division of the Hayden Survey extensively traveled the San Juans during the early boom days. True to the purpose of the survey, they reported on more than the geology, biology, and morphology of the area. In the *Tenth Annual Report of the United States Geological and Geographical Survey of the Territories* (1876), F. M. Endlich observed: "Up to the present time the development of the San Juan mines has been retarded by the want of available capital. The individual miner, however industrious he may be, can not by his own physical labor properly develop a mine." With the mass of humanity swarming into the San Juans came outside capital and a rapidly advancing technology that efficiently extracted and processed the metallic wealth locked within mountains. Despite the legends of Hollywood and anecdotal western histories, the San Juan mining boom was a capital-intensive venture using the best available technology of the day in search of the wealth that helped build a modern industrial nation.

The San Juans produced their share, and more, of colorful characters. Yet, the history of mining in the San Juans and elsewhere increasingly became a drama not of individual actors but of classes and large corporations. What had once been a fluid, open society solidified into an organized industrial hierarchy of workers, hired managers, and absentee owners. One result was the bloody, infamous labor battles that shook the Telluride area and other mining towns in the early decades of the twentieth century.

To unlock the wealth of the San Juans, roads and railroads were needed. The nineteenth-century road builders, engineers, and railroad men blasted routes through the sheer canyons and over the highest ridges in the area, leaving in their wake an incredible if fragile transportation network. Much of their handiwork has vanished, but enough remains or has been restored to satisfy even the most enthusiastic backcountry traveler. Passengers can still travel by steam locomotive along the historic narrow gauge route from Durango to Silverton and tour the high-country crossings over Engineer Mountain,

Cinnamon Pass, Ophir Pass, Imogene Pass, the Million Dollar Highway, and dozens of lesser known routes that lead deep into the San Juans. Then, too, numerous pass routes exist along the edge of the San Juans, which include such famous routes as Cumbres Pass and lesser known yet outstanding trips such as the journey over Stunner and Elwood passes.

No single visit to the San Juans can do justice to the diverse wonders of the area. They are too numerous and are too dependent on seasonal variations. When you visit the San Juan country, linger for a while and leave the least possible evidence of your travels: it is a high and fragile environment that has already suffered sufficiently at the hands of our predecessors.

The abandoned mining town of Alta, located between Ophir and Telluride. Lizard Head and other prominent San Miguel peaks rise in the background. *Courtesy, State of Colorado.*

39 Cumbres Pass

Location: between Antonito, Colorado and Chama, New Mexico

Difficulty: see text

Scenic Quality: lovely area with fine scenic views

Historic Interest: very high

Side Roads: several interesting side trips available

High Point: 10,015 feet

Maps: USFS map of Rio Grande National Forest at 1:125,000

USGS sheet 1 of Conejos County at 1:50,000

Colorado highway map at 1:1,000,000

When we last left the San Juan branch of the Denver & Rio Grande Railway (*see* La Veta Pass in the Sangre de Cristo section), it had crossed the Sangre de Cristo Mountains and the San Luis Valley, reaching the Rio Grande River in 1878. There the railroad company founded the town of Alamosa—land development and real estate speculation contributed substantially to the profits of many nineteenth-century railroads. From Alamosa, D&RG engineers surveyed a route south to Antonito. From Antonito, they laid down fifty tortuous miles of track to reach the summit of Cumbres Pass, which is less than twenty-five miles distant from Antonito.

The Cumbres Pass route was a compromise:

Abandoned Denver and Rio Grande snowshed on the summit of Cumbres Pass.

Old Denver and Rio Grande water tank at Osier.

lower but less direct than taking Stony Pass or another more northerly route to Durango. Moreover, Cumbres Pass was a well-established route from the Rio Grande Basin into the San Juan drainage. The Park View and Ft. Garland Toll Road crossed Cumbres Pass, so that the logistics of transporting work crews and equipment was simplified. But as the D&RG was to learn through the years, the Cumbres Pass area accumulates a substantial snowpack, which, in turn, leads to high maintenance costs and salvage operations to retrieve rolling stock caught in the avalanches that periodically sweep through the area.

Of the original routes over Cumbres Pass, the toll road was the first to succumb; it was replaced in the 1920s by a gravel highway and later a paved highway connecting Antonito and Chama, New Mexico. The narrow gauge Cumbres Pass line survived the demise of the San Juan mines by switching to a variety of other freight, including

lumber, fruit, cattle, sheep, beans, and oil, but in 1951 the Denver and Rio Grande Western discontinued passenger service on its Cumbres Pass route. In 1968, the line from Antonito to Durango was abandoned. But in 1970, the line was reopened when the states of Colorado and New Mexico created joint railroad authorities that purchased the Antonito to Chama portion of the San Juan extension, along with much of the D&RGW's unique inventory of rolling stock. In 1971, the line began operation again as the Cumbres & Toltec Scenic Railroad, which provides four-day-a-week passenger service between Antonito and Chama from June to October.

Starting at the community of Conejos, on the northwest edge of Antonito, a back road traveling along Bighorn Creek approximately parallels the old toll road route. This road, from which numerous side routes diverge, climbs toward Osier Mountain, where it reaches a point higher than Cumbres Pass. It then drops along the toll road route to the town site of Osier, where the tollgate for the wagon road was once located. With the arrival of the Denver & Rio Grande, Osier became a railroad town complete with depot, post office, bunkhouse, saloon, and water tank.

From Osier, the back road travels south in a series of steep curves, then rejoins the main highway, Colorado 17, about two miles east of the Cumbres Pass summit. The railroad tracks, the remains of the old toll road, and the modern highway converge at the summit, where the settlement of Cumbres (known also as Alta) was once located. From the top of Cumbres Pass, the railroad and the modern highway parallel the toll road route to Chama. At the pass summit, a short road runs south to Garcia Lake, and several four-wheel-drive roads travel north into the Rio Grande National Forest. From the Elk Creek Campground, which is about a dozen miles east of the Cumbres Pass summit, on State Highway 17, a good Forest Service road travels to Platero Reservoir, over Stunner Pass, and into the Elwood Pass area, joining US Highway 160 on the east side of Wolf Creek Pass.

Although the backcountry roads in the Cumbres Pass area will provide motorized travelers with an enjoyable touring experience, the Cumbres & Toltec Scenic Railroad trip is the most rewarding and historically authentic route over Cumbres Pass. Not only is the scenery splendid, but nowhere else today is it possible to experience so vividly the difficulties and triumphs of nineteenth-century railroading in the Colorado Rockies. Steam era enthusiasts should plan to linger a while in the Chama, New Mexico, rail yard, where the C&T houses a collection of narrow gauge rolling stock said to be the largest such inventory in North America. The collection includes rotary plows, flangers, water cars, steam engines, and other rarely seen vestiges of a bygone era.

The two best periods to travel the C&T route are early in the season, when the aspen have just leafed and newborn calves are frolicking on the lush subalpine meadows, or in the fall, when the hillsides are glowing with autumn colors. Whatever the time of year, a trip on the Cumbres & Toltec Scenic Railroad is enhanced by obtaining a copy of Doris Osterwald's delightful and informative book, *Ticket to Toltec*, which provides an exhaustive mile-by-mile account of the history and geology of the route.

40 Stunner Pass

Location: between the Alamosa River and
the Conejos River
Difficulty: can be traversed by most smaller,
high-centered passenger cars
Scenic Quality: attractive area with interest-
ing views on the north side of the pass
Historic Interest: modest
Side Roads: a few of interest
High Point: 10,541 feet
Maps: USFS map of Rio Grande National
Forest at 1:125,000
USGS sheet 1 of Conejos County at 1:50,000
Colorado highway map at 1:1,000,000

The need for a pass road over the ridge of
mountains separating the Alamosa River and the
Conejos River drainages arose from the discovery
of ore deposits a short distance above the banks
of the Alamosa River. The site was called, among
other names, Stunner. In 1884, local interests organized the Le Duc and Sanchez Toll Road Company to construct a road from Antonito up the
Conejos River and over the mountains to
Stunner. The Stunner Pass road also served as a
freight route from Platero north to Alamosa and
Del Norte. But Stunner never flourished due to
its relatively isolated location and the lack of
high-grade gold or silver deposits. Summitville,

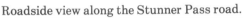
Roadside view along the Stunner Pass road.

February view of the Stunner Pass road to Alamosa.

which had better access to neighboring towns and more extensive mineral resources, remained the principal mining center in the district. In 1890, Stunner acquired a post office, but by the end of the century the mines had already yielded their best ores and the town rapidly declined.

The Stunner Pass road, however, outlasted the usefulness of the mining site for which it was named. The pass route continues to provide access between the upper Conejos River valley and the lovely forest lands to the north of the Alamosa River. Forest Service signs give recognition to the route, and Colorado's highway maps continue to show the location of the road and the pass.

To reach Stunner Pass from the south, journey up the scenic Conejos River valley from Colorado Highway 17 and take a right-hand fork in the road just beyond Platero. The pass road is marked as the route to the Alamosa River. After a short and uneventful climb, the road tops a low summit and becomes substantially rougher and more narrow as it descends to the Alamosa River and the town site of Stunner. Along the north

side of the road are striking volcanic rock formations stained in bright hues of red, orange, and yellow. At the northern base of Stunner Pass, three routes are available: east along the Alamosa River road to Monte Vista or Alamosa; west over Elwood Pass to US Highway 160 and Pagosa Springs (four-wheel-drive is required on this route); or north along the edge of Elwood Pass, through Summitville to Del Norte on US Highway 160. The route from Del Norte to Summitville and over Stunner Pass to Colorado Highway 17 west of Antonito ranks among the longest (about sixty miles) and most scenic of the backcountry pass routes that can be negotiated by passenger cars under good conditions.

The variety of side roads to the north of Stunner Pass is mentioned in the following section on Elwood Pass. On the south side of Stunner Pass are a profusion of hiking trails, most of which intersect in complex looping patterns, and in the vicinity of Platero Reservoir, several interesting side roads lead into the heavily forested countryside on the eastern flank of the San Juan Mountains.

99

41 Elwood Pass

Location: between Del Norte or Alamosa
  and Pagosa Springs
Difficulty: summit can be reached by some
  passenger cars from the east; four-wheel-
  drive required on the west
Scenic Quality: very attractive area with
  exceptional scenery on east side
Historic Interest: moderate
Side Roads: many of scenic and historic
  interest on the east side
High Point: 11,631 feet
Maps: USFS map of Rio Grande National
  Forest at 1:125,000
USFS map of San Juan National Forest at
  1:125,000
USGS sheet 1 of Rio Grande County at 1:50,000
USGS sheet 2 of Mineral County at 1:50,000

Elwood Pass, a high and remote crossing of the Continental Divide to the south of Wolf Creek Pass, was developed in 1878 by the U.S. Army as a road to connect Fort Garland, on the east side of the San Luis Valley, with Fort Lewis in Pagosa Springs. Until the World War I era, when Wolf Creek Pass was established as an automobile route, Elwood Pass remained a well-known crossing point from southern Colorado into the San Juan Basin. During this period, it was the only major pass route between historic Stony Pass, to the north, and the Denver and Rio Grande's Cumbres Pass narrow gauge line along the New Mexico border.

Beginning in the early 1880s, prospectors found extensive deposits of gold, silver, copper, and other minerals at a variety of locations on the east side of Elwood Pass. The most famous and best preserved of the mining camps and town

West side of Elwood Pass road with the Continental Divide in the background.

sites is Summitville, located about three miles northeast of Elwood Pass. Several large mills and numerous cabins still stand at the abandoned site. At its peak in the 1880s, Summitville included nine mills, a newspaper, and more than one dozen saloons. In 1888, a toll road was constructed from Del Norte to Summitville and over a Continental Divide crossing called Summit Pass to the west side of Elwood Pass. Following a period of decline, the Summitville mines reopened in 1935, new ore-handling facilities were constructed, and the population of the town rose to 700, making it then the second largest mining camp in the state.

The appeal of the Elwood Pass area results from the many remaining structures, the extensive network of roads and trails, and most of all, from the very special character of the countryside. There are three different approaches to Elwood Pass: from Del Norte and Summitville to the northeast; the historic eastern route up the Alamosa River; and the western approach along the East Fork of the San Juan River. Each approach is attractive yet because of the terrain is markedly different from the other routes. Then, too, the east side of Elwood Pass is an area of peculiar and striking beauty, a haunting landscape of sculptured forms that particularly in the late afternoon combine with the play of light and shadow to create a unique sense of pastoral charm and otherworldly splendor. Elwood Pass is a high crossing, higher than Berthoud Pass and nearly as high as Loveland Pass, but it exhibits none of the barren and rugged landforms so frequently found along the front range of the Rockies. Instead, volcanic eruptions in the Summitville area created rock that has oxidized to unnatural hues, and the heavy winter snowfalls produce enough moisture to carpet the rolling terrain with an abundance of subalpine vegetation.

Of the three approaches to Elwood Pass, the route from Del Norte on US Highway 160 along the old wagon road to Summitville, now labeled as Rio Grande Road 14, is the most interesting. Beginning by the waters of the Rio Grande, the road travels up a narrow Spanish ranching valley and passes through stands of cottonwood to aspen and then pine forests as it climbs along a Public Service Company power line route into a picturesque alpine landscape to the southeast of Greyback Mountain. After dipping back into a pine forest, the road climbs again to the open meadows near timberline and the remains of

Summitville. To the right is an unmarked road around the north side of Summitville to a high, winding ridge that travels above the broad expanse of Schinzel Flats. About four miles from Summitville, a small sign points the way west to Elwood Pass, a short distance away. Since the final quarter mile of road is rutted and rough, most passenger car travelers must hike to the top of the pass. From the pass summit, four-wheel-drive vehicles can either descend the occasionally steep road on the west side of Elwood Pass, return east along the Alamosa River, or return south over Stunner Pass to the Conejos River. All other motorized travelers must select one of these two eastern routes down from Elwood Pass, but the trip from the pass summit to Stunner Campground (about seven miles) or up by this same route is outstanding in its own right. It offers some fine scenery along with a memorable view of multihued Lookout Mountain and the mineral-stained creeks that wash through the area.

The west side approach to Elwood Pass begins from US Highway 160, below Wolf Creek Pass, at the East Fork road. This scenic eighteen-mile route to the top of the pass travels through a small canyon, then along a lovely ranching valley followed by a sharp fork (which is not labeled) left to a stream crossing and a climb along the hillside above Elwood Creek. Several more steep climbs through a high pine forest lead to the top of the summit ridge. Because neither the west side approach nor the approach from Del Norte is well marked, travelers should be certain to bring a full complement of maps with them. Careful route finding is also essential to explore the extraordinary maze of side roads along the Del Norte–Summitville approach to Elwood Pass or the additional side roads south and east of the pass summit. Intrepid pass road travelers can entertain themselves searching out the route of Summit Pass, which is less than one mile north of Elwood Pass and also the route to Bonito Pass, which can be reached by several trails starting from the east side of Wolf Creek Pass. In addition, a rough but reportedly passable road travels west and then south from the Del Norte to Summitville road over Blowout Pass and terminates on the Alamosa River approach to Elwood Pass and Stunner Pass about a dozen miles east of the Elwood Pass summit. The Blowout Pass route was used in the later years of the nineteenth century to haul freight and ore between Del Norte, Stunner, and Platero.

42 Los Piños Pass

Location: between the Gunnison area and
  Lake City on Colorado 149
Difficulty: can be negotiated by many
  passenger cars under normal conditions
Scenic Quality: attractive with varied country-
  side and fine west side views
Historic Interest: moderate
Side Roads: several interesting routes
  available
High Point: about 10,500 feet
Maps: USFS map of Gunnison National Forest
  at 1:125,000
USGS sheets 1 and 3 of Saguache County
  at 1:50,000
USGS sheet 1 of Hinsdale County at 1:50,000
Colorado highway map at 1:1,000,000

Shadowed aspen on the route to Los Piños Pass.

The Los Piños Pass route probably existed for centuries as a Ute trail between the Lake City area and the Cochetopa Hills passageways into the upper portion of the San Luis Valley. At the time that Hayden's 1877 *Atlas of Colorado* was published, a wagon road branched down Los Piños Creek from the Cochetopa Pass toll road and headed northwest to the Gunnison River at a point several miles beyond the government's Los Piños Indian Agency, established in 1869 when various southern bands of Ute were relocated from the San Luis Valley. From this point, a trail route continued up Los Piños Creek, over a low mountain ridge, and down Cebolla Creek to the Lake City wagon road.

Except that it is wide and smooth enough to accommodate the majority of passenger cars (long and low-slung cars are not advised to attempt the route), the Los Piños Pass route has probably changed little in the past century. It remains a highly scenic byway into the Lake City area. From the east, Los Piños Pass can be reached either by way of Colorado Highway 114 or, in a more leisurely fashion, the Cochetopa Pass road. In either case, the Los Piños Pass route begins about two miles north of the Lower Dome Reservoir and travels past the old Los Piños Indian Agency, which is an attractive Forest Service work center. From there, the road continues along the scenic valley formed by Los Piños Creek and climbs along hillsides to the pass summit. Beyond the summit, a huge sculptured valley unfolds beneath the snowcapped rim of the San Juans. After going through a lovely canyon, the road continues downstream through a popular fishing area for about twelve miles, ending at Colorado Highway 149, just below the summit of Slumgullion Pass. A short distance to the west are more than one-half dozen 14,000-foot peaks, and beyond them, over Engineer and Cinnamon passes, lie Ouray and Silverton.

Although the Los Piños Pass area lacks the grandeur of the high San Juan crossings, it offers pretty, unspoiled countryside, uncrowded campsites, and the opportunity for solitary journeys down meandering side roads and hiking trails. The majority of side roads are located on the east side of the pass, and most of the hiking trails start from the west side of the Los Piños Pass road. About eleven miles east of the summit, a Forest Service road (8EE) branches off from the main pass road (KK14) along Blue Creek and goes toward the high peaks of the La Garita Wilderness before returning to the pass road about one mile east of the summit. From this side road, additional routes branch off toward the Continental Divide. On the west side of the pass, trails lead south to and over the Divide along a ridge where nearly all the major peaks reach above 13,000 feet.

Cebolla Creek canyon on the west side of Los Piños Pass.

43 Owl Creek Pass

Location: between Ridgway on US Highway 550 and Cimarron on US Highway 50
Difficulty: can be negotiated by most passenger cars under good conditions
Scenic Quality: pretty countryside south of the pass with interesting rock formations in the summit area
Historic Interest: slight
Side Roads: variety of routes available on both sides of the pass
High Point: 10,114 feet
Maps: USFS map of Uncompahgre National Forest at 1:125,000
USGS sheet 1 of Ouray County at 1:50,000
USGS sheet 6 of Gunnison County at 1:50,000
USGS sheet 1 of Hinsdale County at 1:50,000
USGS sheet 2 of Montrose County at 1:50,000

The Owl Creek Pass road is a backcountry route between the Uncompahgre Valley and the Gunnison River. The trip over Owl Creek would be little more than a pleasant and relaxing sojourn through some pretty countryside with a good view of the Sneffels Range and the San Juans were it not for one particular feature of the landscape. That feature is the ridge line traversed by Owl Creek Pass. To the north and south of the pass, along Cimarron Ridge, rises a spine of picturesquely sculptured rock offering a nice change of scenery from the massive stone monuments and windswept basins that lie in a semicircular rim to the south of Owl Creek Pass. In place of the grandeur and majesty of the San Juans, the Owl Creek area contains a fanciful progression of rock forms with names like Chimney Rock, Courthouse Mountain, Washboard Rock, Sawtooth Rocks, and Castle Rock.

This peculiar ridge of cleanly cut formations appears to offer technical rock climbers some interesting ascents in an area unscarred by the pitons of previous climbing parties. Since thick stands of aspen line both sides of the pass, the area holds bright prospects for fall aspen watchers who like to enjoy the golden yellow

Chimney Rock and neighboring formations by the summit of Owl Creek Pass.

colors of autumn far from the maddening crowds that descend upon better known spots.

From US Highway 550 by Ridgway, the road to Owl Creek Pass begins at a large highway sign pointing east. It travels through quietly beautiful ranching country, rising into forests of pine and aspen as the route climbs along a gently graded roadway toward the pass summit and several excellent views of Chimney Rock. Beyond the top of Owl Creek Pass, the road descends smoothly along the West Fork of the Cimarron River, then traverses to the Middle Fork of the Cimarron and **winds along the east side of Silver Jack Reservoir. Along this portion of the route, lovely afternoon views emerge from the roadside and the lush vegetation is fed by an irrigation ditch that flows** beside the route. A good dirt road travels from the reservoir through the low, rolling countryside of Wells Basin to US Highway 50 by Curecanti National Receation Area and the Black Canyon of the Gunnison National Monument.

Both sides of Owl Creek Pass offer a variety of side roads. West of the pass, backcountry roads travel up Lou Creek toward Lou Creek Pass, up Deer Creek toward Slagle Pass and South Castle Peak, and along Cow Creek. East of Owl Creek Pass, side roads ascend the West Fork, the Middle Fork, and the East Fork of the Cimarron River. From the end of these roads, hiking trails lead toward Wetterhorn Peak and Uncompahgre Peak, both of which are located on the eastern end of the Uncompahgre Primitive Area.

44 Stony Pass

Location: between Silverton and Creede
Difficulty: four-wheel-drive required
Scenic Quality: varied and dramatic scenery
   of uncommon quality
Historic Interest: very high
Side Roads: many of scenic value and historic
   interest
High Point: **12,588 feet**
Maps: USFS map of Uncompahgre National
   Forest at 1:125,000
USFS map of Rio Grande National Forest
   at 1:125,000
USGS single sheet of San Juan County at
   1:50,000
USGS sheet 2 of Hinsdale County at 1:50,000
USGS sheet 1 of Mineral County at 1:50,000

Aerial tramway along the route from Stony Pass to Cunningham Gulch.

Between the headwaters of the Rio Grande River and the San Juan country stands the Continental Divide. For many centuries, the Utes crossed this barrier along a relatively low route known as Weminuche Pass (10,629 feet), which connected the Rio Grande with the Los Piños River and the Durango area. Another crossing, Hunchback Pass, higher and about a dozen miles farther west, led from a tributary of the Rio Grande over the Divide and down Vallecito Creek into the same area. But the San Juan mining boom began not in Durango, but fifty miles farther up the Animas River in the Baker Park area just north of Silverton. Another pass route was needed.

That new pass route, known then as Rio Grande Pass or Cunningham Pass and now as Stony Pass, traveled up to the very headwaters of the Rio Grande, crossed over the Continental Divide, then dropped precipitously down to Cunningham Gulch about two miles from Howardsville and only six miles from Silverton. The distance from Del Norte, then a regional supply center, to Silverton by way of this route was about 110 miles, so Stony Pass became the gateway into the Silverton area until 1882, when Denver & Rio Grande narrow gauge locomotives began chugging up the Animas River gorge from Durango. In 1874, the San Juan Division of the Hayden Survey crossed Stony and Weminuche passes. The 1877 Hayden *Atlas of Colorado* shows the Stony Pass crossing as a wagon road, but at the time that it was traveled by Hayden's San Juan Division, the upper portion of the route was barely a burro trail. By 1879, a wagon road had been constructed over a crossing slightly north of the earlier gateway, but no route over

Stony Pass could compete with the railroad. The Stony Pass road was largely abandoned, and only in the last twenty years has it seen much use as a scenic tourist route.

To reach Stony Pass from the west, the shortest route to the summit, take US Highway 550 to Silverton. At the north end of town, continue on the paved road northeast up the Animas River about three and one-half miles to Howardsville. At Howardsville, travel south one and one-half miles on the improved road leading up historic Cunningham Gulch and turn left on an unmarked side road. Turn right again at a small sign indicating the route to Stony Pass. Starting at this point, the road climbs very steeply, giving passengers with the courage to look back excellent views of Galena Mountain and Cunningham Gulch. After one of the longest sustained climbs of any Colorado pass road, the route emerges into an alpine valley and ascends more gently to the barren summit, which overlooks the headwaters of the Rio Grande. The east side of the pass route is not so steep but certainly ranks among the longest such roads in Colorado. From the top of Stony Pass, it is a journey of about thirty miles to Colorado Highway 149, followed by several more miles of unpaved highway driving. However, the route is highly scenic, and from Lost Trail Campground, at the end of Rio Grande Reservoir, it is a relatively easy trip along the northern border of the Weminuche Wilderness.

No trip to Stony Pass is complete without sufficient time to explore the side roads and hiking trails that abound on both sides of the pass summit. Many of the side roads on the west side of Stony Pass are described in the sections on nearby Cinnamon Pass and the Engineer Mountain passes. Additional side roads exist in the vicinity of Middleton, two miles north of Howardsville, along Minnie Gulch and Maggie Gulch, and along the Eureka Gulch road that begins at the abandoned town site of Eureka, three miles north of Howardsville. At the north edge of Silverton, by the start of the Animas Forks road, an improved dirt road suitable for most passenger cars leads up Cement Creek to Gladstone, site of the massive Gold King mine and once a community of 2,000 people. From Gladstone, four-wheel-drive roads climb high into the surrounding mountains.

The east side of Stony Pass offers a wide variety of additional side roads. About five miles below the summit, a road up Bear Creek travels to the site of Beartown, an 1890s mining camp, and to Kite Lake, located a short distance from Hunchback Pass. Other side roads travel to Heart Lake, Black Mountain Lake, Hermit Lake, South Lazy U Reservoir, Regan Lake, and Santa Maria Reservoir. In addition, hiking trails traverse the countryside both to the north and south of the road. Many of these trails lead over unnamed crossings of the Continental Divide into the San Juan and Gunnison national forests, and since many of the routes intersect, hikers can choose from among a wide variety of paths through this little used but lovely countryside near the headwaters of the Rio Grande River.

45 Cinnamon Pass

Location: between Lake City and Ouray
Difficulty: four-wheel-drive required
Scenic Quality: very high along the entire route
Historic Interest: very high
Side Roads: many of exceptional scenic and
   historic interest
High Point: 12,620 feet
Maps: USFS map of Uncompahgre National
   Forest at 1:125,000
USGS sheet 1 of Hinsdale County at 1:50,000
USGS sheet 2 of Ouray County at 1:50,000
USGS single sheet of San Juan County at
   1:50,000

When Charles Baker made his famous trek of 1860 to the San Juans, his route led over Cinnamon Pass and down the Animas River. Fourteen years later, the same Hayden Survey party that explored Stony Pass traveled the Cinnamon Pass route to then well-known Baker's Park, where a mining boom that would soon reach immense proportions was getting underway. The men of the Hayden Survey did not think the Cinnamon Pass crossing a likely spot for the construction of a wagon road into the San Juans. It was too high and steep a route to be reliable.

But there were no gentle pass routes into the heart of the San Juans from the east, and the miners in that district, like the bumblebee unaware of scientific pronouncements that it was aerodynamically incapable of flying, soon proceeded to install a wagon road from Lake City over Cinnamon Pass to the Animas Valley. The road, built under the direction of Enos Hotchkiss, was completed in 1877. It served as an important link between the Lake City and Animas Valley area until the coming of the railroads and declining ore production doomed the crossing as a principal route over the San Juans. But the east side of the Cinnamon Pass road, leading to the mining town of Whitecross and the mines high in American Basin and Cinnamon Mountain, received regular use into the twentieth century.

Even today, the Cinnamon Pass road is a useful route. One August day I rented a jeep in Lake City and crossed over North Engineer Pass on my way west to Ouray and Imogene Pass. I had planned to return to Lake City by way of Cinna-

Animas Forks and the upper Animas Valley from the Cinnamon Pass road. *Courtesy, Dick Hart.*

Abandoned tower near the summit of Cinnamon Pass.

mon Pass, which is a thirty-five-mile trip from the Mineral Creek turnoff on US Highway 550. But I did not reach the turnoff until nearly sundown. Not wanting to attempt a night trip over Cinnamon Pass in a rented jeep, I elected to take the main highway route north to the Gunnison River and back down the Lake Fork to Lake City. It was a 140-mile trip that could otherwise have been accomplished in one-quarter the distance.

The east side approach to Cinnamon Pass begins on Colorado Highway 149, about two miles south of Lake City, at the route to Lake San Cristobal. A good graveled road passes beside the lake and begins climbing up the Lake Fork of the Gunnison River to the site of Whitecross. This portion of the route offers excellent south side views of Redcloud and Sunshine peaks. Beyond Whitecross, the road emerges into an expanse of lovely alpine terrain and an impressive summit view, followed by a short scenic descent of less than two miles. The road ends at a junction along the Animas River a short distance above the abandoned town of Animas Forks. Two miles north of this junction on the Animas River road is the turnoff to Mineral Creek, Ouray, and Lake City via Engineer Mountain. The route south from the junction leads to Howardsville and Stony Pass or, by continuing south another three miles, to Silverton and US Highway 550. The west side approach to Cinnamon Pass from Ouray to Silverton is identical to the Engineer Mountain routes except that the turnoff to the summit climb is located two miles farther south on the road up the Animas Valley.

A trip over Cinnamon Pass can be combined with a return trip by way of Engineer Mountain to Lake City or over Stony Pass to Creede. In addition, many side roads of interest are located in the vicinity of Cinnamon Pass. Two miles west of the Mill Creek Campground on the east side of the pass, a back road travels up Cottonwood Creek. About two miles below the summit of Cinnamon Pass, a short but scenic road ascends into spectacular American Basin, which is rimmed on the east by Handies Peak, a fourteener. In addition, from the summit of the pass, a short side road travels north along the ridge, while another road leads south to the large Tabasco mine, once owned by the sauce manufacturing company of the same name.

Still another side road of special interest to the east of the pass starts from the Cinnamon Pass road about one mile east of Mill Creek Campground and travels up Wager Gulch to a high and remote Continental Divide crossing at the site of Carson, where a large alpine mining camp existed for about twenty years. Though I have not traveled the route, my friend and back-country touring companion, Dick Hart, took a four-wheel-drive vehicle over the crossing, which he calls Carson Pass. He reports that it is a rough but spectacular journey to a well preserved ghost town located in a dramatic setting. A wagon road constructed in 1887 once connected Carson with Creede. This latter route along Lost Trail Creek is not negotiable by motor vehicle according to reports, but an alternate route to the east that travels along the north side of Heart Lake to South Clear Creek Falls Campground on Colorado Highway 149 may be open to four-wheel-drive vehicles for the entire distance from Carson to Creede.

46, 47 Engineer Mountain Passes (Yvonne and Engineer Passes)

Location: between Lake City and Ouray
Difficulty: four-wheel-drive required for summit portion on both sides
Scenic Quality: outstanding
Historic Interest: very high
Side Roads: many of exceptional interest
High Points: about 12,800 feet and 12,750 feet
Maps: USFS map of Uncompahgre National Forest at 1:125,000
USGS sheet 1 of Hinsdale County at 1:50,000
USGS sheet 2 of Ouray County at 1:50,000
USGS single sheet of San Juan County at 1:50,000

The Engineer Mountain crossing between Lake City and the Animas River is not the oldest, or highest, or even the most spectacular pass road in the San Juans. But it is the best known and most often traveled of the four-wheel-drive San Juan passes because it is an accessible route to a fabled mining district in a landscape of striking beauty. Stony Pass is an older route, and Imogene Pass offers scenery of more stunning grandeur. But the trip up Henson Creek and around the side of Engineer Mountain to Mineral Point and Animas Forks best captures for modern-day travelers a sense of what it must have been like a century ago when an army of fortune seekers swarmed through the San Juans, bringing a frontier civilization to the holy land of the Utes.

By the time Otto Mears completed his wagon road over Engineer Mountain in August 1877, the San Juan boom was already underway. Ouray and Silverton were well-established communities, and Lake City was an important enough town that Susan B. Anthony visited it that year to preach the gospel of women's suffrage. Thousands of miners were toiling in the mines and mills around Capital City, American Flats, Mineral Point, and a dozen other locations. The Engineer Mountain pass road allowed stagecoach passengers, freight wagons, and mule trains to

The Animas Valley above the town of Animas Forks. The side road visible on the left leads over Cinnamon Pass. *Courtesy,* Dick Hart.

travel conveniently—more or less—between Lake City, Ouray, and Silverton. By 1880, the Rocky Mountain Stage and Express Company was providing daily coach service between Lake City and Animas Forks by way of Engineer Mountain.

The Engineer Mountain crossing actually encompasses two separate passes. The traditional route, known properly as Engineer Pass, switchbacked up the east face of Engineer Mountain just south of the summit and descended the west side in a steep, direct route. The contemporary route, known in some circles as Yvonne Pass but loosely referred to also as Engineer Pass, travels around the north side of Engineer Mountain and descends the west side on a more gentle but very exposed shelf road that joins the Engineer Pass road about one mile west of the summit.

The east side route to both crossings starts at the south end of Lake City on Colorado Highway 149. A good gravel road travels west up Henson Creek, giving excellent views of Wetterhorn Peak and Uncompahgre Peak to the north and, to the

south, Redcloud Peak and behind it Sunshine Peak (all fourteeners). Most smaller passenger cars can navigate the route to Capital City or Rose Cabin. From Rose Cabin, the road climbs more steeply through the alpine terrain above American Flats to the summit. From the top of North Engineer Pass, the Animas Valley comes into view, surrounded by a vast wonderland of high peaks reaching out in every direction to the horizon. The west side shelf road, though exposed, is wider than several other such routes and is perfectly safe to travel by four-wheel-drive vehicle so long as the road is dry and caution is used. The shelf road descends to the upper end of the Animas Valley. From this point, a traveler must decide among several routes. A road to the west down Mineral Creek leads to US Highway 550, the Million Dollar Highway, about three miles north of Ouray. The main road through the valley travels past the Cinnamon Pass cutoff, and the route back to Lake City goes past the site of Animas Forks and to a high-quality graveled

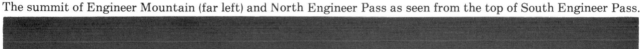

The summit of Engineer Mountain (far left) and North Engineer Pass as seen from the top of South Engineer Pass.

road that leads to Howardsville and Silverton. The Cunningham Gulch road at Howardsville leads over Stony Pass, offering additional circle trip opportunities. From Ouray, the quickest approach to Engineer Mountain is by way of Mineral Creek, but the longer route from Silverton up the Animas River past Howardsville and Eureka is a delightful and historic trip that adds to the pleasure of the journey. Most smaller passenger cars can navigate the Animas Valley road to Animas Forks and the base of Engineer Mountain.

The South Engineer Pass route is nearly identical to its northerly neighbor. To explore this alternate route from the east, take the unmarked side road to the south from the North Engineer Pass road at the base of Engineer Mountain. Be advised, however, that the south side pass road is very narrow in spots and may be blocked by rock slides along its switchbacked route to the top. From the west side, the South Engineer Pass road starts at an unmarked junction about one mile below the south side summit. Although the route is a bit rough, it can be readily negotiated by four-wheel-drive vehicles. From the top of the south side pass, a road extends to the 13,218-foot-high summit of Engineer Mountain, affording an even better view of the surrounding mountainscape.

The Engineer Mountain area is laced with additional side roads along with the routes already described. One of the best known of these roads begins just east from the summit of North Engineer Pass and descends from the dizzy heights of Engineer Mountain to the alpine expanse of American Flats, a high and lonely basin where the mining camp called Engineer City once stood. Another of the exciting side roads in the area begins on the Animas Valley road about two miles below the summit of North Engineer Pass and travels over Denver Pass, a 12,200-foot crossing that would be a well-known route in its own right were it located in a less spectacular area. From Denver Pass, the road leads to Mineral Point, an isolated mining town that once boasted a population that approached one thousand. From Mineral Point, the road drops a short distance to the Mineral Creek road, joining it about four miles from US Highway 550.

48 Imogene Pass

Location: between Ouray and Telluride
Difficulty: four-wheel-drive required/special
   caution recommended
Scenic Quality: outstanding with magnificent
   views on both sides
Historic Interest: high
Side Roads: a few of special scenic and
   historic interest
High Point: 13,114 feet
Maps: USFS map of Uncompahgre National
   Forest at 1:125,000
USGS sheet 2 of Ouray County at 1:50,000
USGS sheet 3 of San Miguel County at
   1:50,000

Imogene Pass is in many respects the San Juan equivalent of Pearl Pass in the Elk Range. It is the highest, toughest, and most spectacular of the drivable San Juan crossings; a challenging road through wildly beautiful countryside connecting two fabled mining towns. Both routes are only for seasoned backcountry motorists, and both provide ample visual rewards to those who venture across them.

The Imogene Pass crossing was developed at a later date than many of the other San Juan crossings. The two principal mines along the Imogene Pass road—the Camp Bird, located above Ouray, and the Tomboy, perched above Telluride—were constructed after the initial burst of mining activity. The lower portions of the Imogene Pass road served to supply these two famous mines. The Camp Bird mine, once owned by Thomas Walsh before he sold it to an English syndicate in 1902 for $5.2 million, ranks among the most productive gold mines in Colorado history. The Tomboy, which the Rothchilds of London purchased in 1897 for $2 million, was among the best known and most notorious mines in the Telluride area because of the violent labor struggles that occurred there in the early twentieth century. The two mines were connected below ground by a network of tunnels and along the surface by the Imogene Pass road. When the Western Federation of Miners won its first strike in 1901, the nonunion labor force beat a hasty retreat by way of Imogene Pass. Following World War I, the Tomboy Gold Mines Company of Telluride purchased a number of mining claims by the town of Sneffels, above the Camp Bird

Site of the Tomboy mine with Imogene Pass in the background. *Courtesy, Dick Hart.*

The summit of Imogene Pass with Chicago Peak and Sneffels Range peaks in the background.

mine, and the Imogene Pass road carried a heavy volume of traffic between the two areas. A high-voltage electric transmission line built by L. L. Nunn, the first alternating current, long-distance line ever constructed, once stretched across Imogene Pass to the Camp Bird area but has since been removed.

From the east, the road to Imogene Pass begins just south of Ouray on US Highway 550 at the turnoff to the Camp Bird mine. After a five-mile journey up dramatic Canyon Creek road, the route swings left across a stream and travels along a very rough road through a wooded area above the Camp Bird and Upper Camp Bird mines. Emerging near timberline, the road enters an imposing valley that leads to Imogene Basin and a rough, steep climb that ends with the final shelf road far above timberline. From the summit of Imogene Pass, the view is as spectacular as the route to the top. To the north is Chicago Peak, and beyond it rises Mt. Sneffels, "Queen of the San Juans." West of the high ridge, which is best viewed from a short hike south toward Telluride Peak, is the Tomboy mine and the spectacular valley leading down Savage Creek to Telluride. The west side of the pass road switchbacks down to Savage Basin and travels along a length of shelf route past the Tomboy mine to Telluride and Colorado Highway 145. Portions of the shelf road are narrow and subject to erosion and may require a bit of impromptu construction for safe passage even by narrow-track vehicles. The route between Telluride and Savage Basin provides unparalleled views of Ingram Falls, the road to Black Bear Pass, and Bridal Veil Falls.

The side roads available from the western end of Imogene Pass are discussed in the following descriptions of Black Bear and Ophir passes. However, travelers wishing to take a spectacular circle route from US Highway 550 can start and return to the Million Dollar Highway via Imogene Pass and Ophir Pass. On the east side of Imogene Pass, a well-known and scenic side road travels north from the Canyon Creek road five miles above the Camp Bird mine and leads to the abandoned mining town of Sneffels and up Sneffels Creek toward Yankee Boy Basin. From this basin, a trail leads over Blue Lakes Pass near Mt. Sneffels to the East Fork of Dallas Creek and an improved road that ends at Colorado Highway 62 west of Ridgway. This route over the Sneffels Range was once a four-wheel-drive road but reportedly is now a hiking trail only. The Yankee Boy Basin route over Blue Lakes Pass was the approach used by the San Juan Division of the Hayden Survey for the first recorded ascent of Mt. Sneffels in September 1874.

114

49 Black Bear Pass

Location: between Red Mountain Pass on
  US Highway 550 and Telluride
Difficulty: four-wheel-drive required/extreme
  caution and cool composure mandatory on
  west side
Scenic Quality: outstanding with dramatic
  views on west side
Historic Interest: moderate
Side Roads: a few of exceptional scenic value
High Point: about 12,840 feet
Maps: USFS map of Uncompahgre National
  Forest at 1:125,000
USGS single sheet of San Juan County at
  1:50,000
USGS sheet 3 of San Miguel County at 1:50,000

Famed first as a mining town and now as a resort area, Telluride has always been known for its awesome physical setting. Telluride rests in a narrow valley blocked on the east by a massive ridge of mountains. Rising 4,000 feet above the town is Ingram Peak, its majestic west face framed on either side by towering waterfalls. Above the waterfalls are alpine basins leading to still higher peaks, and etched into the west face of Ingram Peak is one of the most awesome roads in the San Juan Mountains or, for that matter, anywhere in the American Rockies.

That road is the Black Bear Pass route, which connects Black Bear mine, situated 12,500 feet up on a flank of Telluride Peak, with the Million Dollar Highway at the top of Red Mountain Pass and with Telluride below. In addition to serving the Black Bear mine, the road provided access to more than a dozen other mines located above Ingram Basin and along the sides of Ajax Peak. The route also connected the early hydroelectric generating station above Bridal Veil Falls with Telluride.

Beginning at an intentionally unmarked side road that starts just south from the top of Red

Imogene Pass road view of Black Bear Pass route framed by Ingram Falls and Bridal Veil Falls.

Ingram Falls and Ajax Peak from the hydroelectric plant at the top of Bridal Veil Falls. Bridal Veil Creek is in the foreground. A portion of the Black Bear Pass road is visible in the background. *Courtesy, State of Colorado.*

Mountain Pass, the route climbs steeply to Mineral Basin and crosses the ridge south of Trico Peak. After reaching the summit, it traverses to the north above Imogene Lake to the Black Bear mine. The road then descends through Ingram Basin to Ingram Falls and continues down a spectacular series of switchbacks to Bridal Veil Falls, past the Idarado mine, the side of Pandora, and on to Telluride. Along the west side of the route are sufficient remains of nineteenth- and early twentieth-century mines, mills, tramways, power stations, and other artifacts to entertain even the most ardent student of early western mining technology.

Unfortunately, the west side of the route also includes a stretch of roadway down Ingram Peak that is treacherously narrow, steep, off-camber, and unstable. When I visited Telluride in August 1978, the owner of a jeep rental service told me that the Black Bear Pass road had claimed eight lives in the previous six years and, despite better graded switchbacks, the route continues to provide real hazards to both drivers and their vehicles. It is a one-way route *only*, down from the US 550 side, and should be attempted only by experienced and cool drivers of short, narrow track four-wheel-drive vehicles. Local jeep rental companies forbid the use of their vehicles on the Black Bear Pass road and during the 1986 season a misguided visitor, attempting to go uphill on the road from Telluride, became so panicked that other persons had to turn the vehicle around and drive it back to town.

From Telluride, the Black Bear road is safely negotiable by most smaller passenger cars past the base of Bridal Veil Falls, the highest waterfall in Colorado, and up several steps of the switchback road to the top of the falls. At this point, the road crosses an avalanche chute that normally leaves snow accumulations that last well into the summer months. But the view from above the falls is well worth the trip: below lies Telluride, and above, Ingram Creek tumbles over the edge of the basin and cascades down the mountainside to the San Miguel River. At the top of the falls, a four-wheel-drive route, now closed, travels along the creek and deep into the magnificent Bridal Veil Basin, rimmed by a wall of 13,000-foot peaks and studded with alpine lakes. From the head of the basin, a route that perhaps may be negotiated by motor vehicles tops a 13,000-foot ridge and drops down Chapman Gulch to the Ophir Pass road about one mile west of the Ophir Pass summit. The east side of the Black Bear Pass road, from US Highway 550 through Mineral Basin and over the pass to the Black Bear mine and into Ingram Basin, is an impressive journey and offers the opportunity for one side trip of special note.

From the Black Bear Pass road in Ingram Basin, a side road to the north switchbacks up the flank of Ajax Peak, ending at a point about one thousand feet above the basin and some four thousand feet higher than Telluride. To complement this view, a traveler can hike a short distance to the top of the ridge and gaze down on Savage Basin and the road leading up to Imogene Pass, which is less than a mile distant from the top of Ajax Peak.

50 Ophir Pass

Location: between Silverton and Telluride
Difficulty: requires high-centered truck or
   passenger car with good traction to reach
   the summit/caution advised on west side
Scenic Quality: very high with impressive
   summit and west side views
Historic Interest: considerable
Side Roads: several of high historic and scenic
   interest on west side
High Point: about 11,789 feet
Maps: USFS map of San Juan National Forest
   at 1:125,000
USFS map of Uncompahgre National Forest
   at 1:125,000
USGS single sheet of San Juan County at
   1:50,000
USGS sheet 3 of San Miguel County at 1:50,000

Although not quite so high or famous as some of the other central San Juan pass routes, Ophir Pass was a well-used route in its day and is still a popular shortcut between Silverton and Telluride during the summer months. Originally

opened as a pass road in the middle 1870s, the Ophir Pass route was converted to a toll road in 1880 and provided access from Silverton and the surrounding area to the mining camps around Ophir and Telluride. With the arrival of Otto Mears' railroad in 1890 and 1891 from Silverton through Ophir to Ouray and Telluride, the need for Ophir Pass diminished, though it remained a time-saving wagon route that drastically reduced the distance from Silverton to the Ophir area and Telluride.

The modern-day Ophir Pass road begins on US Highway 550 about five and one-half miles north of Silverton and about an equal distance from the summit of Red Mountain Pass. The road climbs through pretty countryside in the Middle Mineral Creek area to a rocky summit framed on each side by 13,000-foot peaks (Lookout Peak on the north and South Lookout Peak on the south). On a clear day, the summit view to the west is worth the trip unto itself. Ahead lies a lush valley formed by the Howard Fork of the San Miguel River, and beyond the valley is the San Miguel Range, topped by the volcanic neck of Lizard Head and a trio of fourteeners: Mt. Wilson, Wil-

The view from Ophir Pass looking west toward the Ophir Needles, center background, and Wilson Peak. *Courtesy, Dick Hart.*

The author on a July outing at the summit of Ophir Pass. *Courtesy, Dick Hart.*

son Peak, and El Diente Peak.

The route leading west from the summit is a shelf road cut into a talus slope. It is better graded and not so narrow as the fearsome shelf roads on Black Bear Pass or Pearl Pass, but like all shelf roads, it must be treated with an appropriate measure of caution even under ideal traveling conditions. Part way down and many hundred feet below the road appears a bright speck among the dark boulders; this wrecked automobile should serve as a grim reminder of what could happen in a moment of carelessness.

At the foot of Ophir Pass is the town of Old Ophir, and about two miles farther down the road is Ophir. These two communities, which sprang up in the mid 1870s, rank among the most famous of the now abandoned, or nearly so, Colorado mining towns. On the outskirts of Old Ophir is a cemetery worth visiting, and just beyond Ophir is the site of the legendary Ophir Loop, a double loop of elevated railroad track built on trestles nearly ten stories high in places. This feat of nineteenth-century engineering wizardry was constructed by that ubiquitous road builder turned railroad entrepreneur, Otto Mears, to reduce the grade on his Rio Grande Southern line as the

tracks climbed toward the summit of Lizard Head Pass.

In addition to the two Ophir towns, the west side of the Ophir Pass road offers a number of sights. At Old Ophir, a side road winds up the side of Silver Mountain through an area that once saw intense mining activity. About one mile north of Ophir, on Colorado Highway 145, a well-known scenic road extends to Alta, where the remains of a mining town are very much in evidence, to the Alta Lakes, and along Boomrang Road back to State Highway 145. Also by Ophir, an improved dirt road travels along the South Fork of the San Miguel River through the former mining towns of Ames and Ilium before joining State Highway 145. From this South Fork road, other side roads go west up Sunshine Mountain and toward Wilson Peak. From Telluride, intrepid travelers can return over Imogene Pass to Ouray or more sedately back to Silverton by way of Red Mountain Pass.

The Ophir Pass area also provides access to a number of good hiking trails that lead into the surrounding National Forests. For a description of these trails, see Ormes' *Guide to the Colorado Mountains.*

A high jeep road in the San Juan Mountains.

A tranquil scene on the Uncompahgre Plateau south of Columbine Pass.

West Spanish Peak as seen from near La Veta.

Part Six
Addendum
A Dozen and More Roads to Travel

The first edition of *The Colorado Pass Book* emphatically stated that it was not a definitive guide to every backcountry pass road in Colorado. Nor does this second edition pretend to be definitive. But after some six years of additional Colorado exploration and research, I have journeyed over more pass roads and learned of still more routes to explore. The list is not yet complete and I hope it never will be. But it continues to grow with every season of high country travel.

The pass roads presented in this Addendum are less likely to be household names than many of the routes previously described in the book, but they are no less scenic, less interesting or less enjoyable to travel. These additional roads range from relatively low elevation routes to a few towering trips far above timberline; from obscure routes to one of the best known backcountry pass roads in Colorado; from the Front Range mountains with a view of the eastern plains to far-flung locations in the San Juan mountains and the canyon and plateau country along the Utah border.

What these passes have in common is, indeed, their diversity of place, of terrain, of difficulty to traverse, and the diversity of experiences that they yield. That is as it should be. If there exists any common thread in the fabric of Colorado, from the short grass prairies of the high plains to the alpine countryside rising above timberline to the slickrock formations of its desert southwest, Colorado is a landscape of contrasts and variation—not just a picture-pretty postcard scene in the mountains.

These dozen and more pass roads to travel are offered simply as an additional tribute to the variety and the vastness that is Colorado, where travelers can lose themselves for days in but a single county.

51 Fall River Pass

Location: in Rocky Mountain National Park between Estes Park and Grand Lake
Difficulty: can be negotiated by most two-wheel drive vehicles under good conditions/ inquire with the Park Service on roadway conditions
Scenic Quality: very high
Historic Interest: moderate
Side Roads: several other National Park Service routes available in the area
High Point: 11,796 feet
Maps: NPS map of Rocky Mountain National Park
USFS map of Roosevelt National Forest at 1:125,000
USGS sheet 3 of Larimer County at 1:50,000

When Rocky Mountain National Park was established in 1915, this vast expanse of high country wilderness contained no through roads across the Continental Divide between the east and west sides of the Park. Two years earlier, in September of 1913, members of the Estes Park Protective and Improvement Association had convinced the State of Colorado to build a road over the Continental Divide with convict labor from Colorado State Penitentiary. But it proved to be a seven year project to dig, blast and grade a road up the Fall River and over Fall River Pass. Finally, in 1920, the National Park Service proudly announced the opening of the Fall River Road across the top of the Park and the number of visitors to the area soared.

The Fall River Road soon proved to be a mixed blessing, however. The narrow, winding roadway, with one steep series of switchbacks near the summit, was more than a match for some of the motor cars of that era. The Park Service also found itself burdened with massive snow removal costs to open the road at the start of the visitor season. In 1921, it took more than a month and two tons of dynamite to clear drifts that were

An early winter view below Fall River Pass in Rocky Mountain National Park.

124

nearly one-quarter mile long and twenty-five feet deep. Park Service officials soon began to contemplate a new route to the top of the Continental Divide. So in 1926, the Bureau of Public Roads started to survey another roadway to the top. This route was along the more open and exposed corridor of Trail Ridge. Construction of the new road began late in 1929 with a work crew of nearly 200 men. Four years and two contractors later (one working from the east side and the other from the west side), the new road opened. With a width of twenty-four feet and no grade in excess of seven percent, Trail Ridge Road provided travelers with quick, easy access to the top of the Park across a route that offered sweeping alpine views that still startle and impress visitors.

The new road, however, was not without its problems. A previously pristine stretch of fragile alpine landscape was opened to intensive recreational use. And once it was paved and populated with modern high powered autos that did not need to crawl up the route in a low gear, Trail Ridge Road became a mountain superhighway that transported visitors from scenic vantage point to scenic vantage point in splendid isolation from the landscape.

The Fall River Pass road, which the Park Service still maintains as a backroad alternative to Trail Ridge, remains today what it has always been: a winding, leisurely route through the woods that emerges at timberline into the alpine splendors of Rocky Mountain National Park. Particularly for those Park visitors who are traveling to the top of the Park and then returning to the east, the Fall River Road is the ideal route up (it is one way only, upbound).

To reach Fall River Pass by way of this historic and scenic route, take US Highway 34 west from Estes Park, branching off on the old road at the far end of Horseshoe Park, by the Endovalley Picnic Area. From this 8,500-foot starting point, the Fall River road climbs by Chasm Falls and Willow Park, ascends a series of switchback turns and emerges from the trees at Marmot Point before joining the paved highway at the 11,796-foot-high summit of Fall River Pass, where a ranger station and the visitor center are located. From this high point on the road, the highway descends along Medicine Bow Curve to the 10,758-foot-high crossing of the Continental Divide at Milner Pass.

Because the Fall River Pass road is located in a National Park, no side roads are available for additional motorized exploration. But the Fall River Road does offer one unusual hiking experience. From the top of the switchbacks, above Willow Park, a hiking trail leads north about one-quarter mile to Chapin Pass; the modest elevation gain of some 150 feet makes this perhaps the easiest pass hike in Colorado. From Chapin Pass, the trail descends along Chapin Creek and the Cache la Poudre River on the west side of the Mummy Range.

A wide variety of other hiking passes are located in Rocky Mountain National Park. South of Milner Pass on US 34, Sprague Pass, Ptarmigan Pass, Andrews Pass, Stone Man Pass and Boulder-Grand Pass all cut across the Continental Divide inside the Park. But there exists one other pass road entrance into the Park. From Colorado Highway 14 about four miles east of the summit of Cameron Pass, a well-maintained Forest Service Road winds around Flat Top Mountain to Long Draw Reservoir and the Park boundary. From the road closure near the Park entrance, it is a short hike to the summit of La Poudre Pass. From there a trail leads south to the site of Lulu City, a short-lived mining town encompassed within the Park borders. Platted in 1883 and named in honor of the founder's daughter, Lulu Burnett, Lulu City once stood along a wagon road that served a variety of mining camps and supply towns in the area.

52, 53 Browns and Breakneck passes

Location: west of US Highway 285 near
  Fairplay
Difficulty: four-wheel-drive required
Scenic Quality: quite attractive with excellent
  Mosquito Range views to the west
Historic Interest: moderate
Side Roads: several of considerable interest
High Point: 11,372 feet (Browns Pass) and
  10,910 feet (Breakneck Pass)
Maps: USFS map of Pike National Forest at
  1:125,000
USGS sheet 1 of Park County at 1:50,000

The town of Fairplay, also called Fairplay
Diggings, Platte City and South Park City, was
established on the far western rim of South Park
in 1859 by miners disgruntled with the greed of
the mining community in Tarryall (*see* No. 54,
LaSalle Pass). The Fairplay area itself soon
emerged as a more extensive mining district than
the Tarryall site, as rich silver and gold deposits
were unearthed along an arc on the east flank of
the Mosquito Range from Mount Lincoln and Mt.

Bross down the range to Mr. Sherman (all fourteen thousand foot peaks).

The most southerly of the mining camps
that sprang up in the area were along Fourmile
Creek, a drainage leading up to the flanks of Mt.
Sherman (14,036 feet in elevation) and Mt.
Sheridan (13,748 feet). The largest towns along
this route were Leavick and Horseshoe, the latter
also known as Doran and East Leadville. Once a
thriving community with a peak population estimated at 800 persons, Horseshoe and the large
mines that supported it have long since been
abandoned. Indeed, few people ever visit the area
today, except on warm summer weekends, despite
the attractive countryside and an extensive network of roads.

Several miles south of Horseshoe, access into
the high mountains of the Mosquito range is
blocked by a series of peaks called Sheep Mountain (and adjacent Lamb Mountain to the west),
Sheep Ridge and Round Hill. Browns Pass gives
access into the valley below the Mosquito Range
at a near-timberline crossing between Sheep
Mountain and the northern flank of Sheep Ridge
while Breakneck Pass skirts a lower, wooded

Looking westward to the Mosquito Range from the summit of Browns Pass.

crossing between the south side of Sheep Ridge and Round Hill. Both passes lead to the same location; the moist and secluded meadowlands of Sheep Park and Twelvemile Creek, but each takes a different route around Sheep Ridge to reach that location.

To find Browns Pass, and also Breakneck Pass, although an alternate route to Breakneck Pass is preferred, take US Highway 285 to about three miles south of its junction with Colorado Highway 9 (or about four miles south of Fairplay) and turn west on Park County Road 20. Then several miles later turn left on Road 176, which is the start of a short but rather steep and rough ascent to Browns Pass. The pass summit is marked by a small Forest Service sign announcing the site. From the pass summit, visitors are afforded a stunning view of 13,898-foot-high Horseshoe Mountain and Peerless Mountain to its north. From Browns Pass the road continues west in a steep, rough descent to Sheep Park on a route along which vehicle travelers should proceed at their own risk.

Perhaps the best route to Breakneck Pass starts not from US Highway 285 but a southern approach route from the Weston Pass road (*see* No. 7). From US Highway 285 about one mile south of the turn-off for Browns Pass, go west on the Weston Pass road, Park County Road 5, and about four miles up that road turn north on Road 175, marked by a sign as the route to Breakneck Pass. The road climbs smoothly up a hillside along the edge of South Park then travels through narrow meadowlands and up a steep wooded section bordered with aspen and continues to a beautifully forested intersection just below the summit of Breakneck Pass. This road, which intersects the Breakneck Pass route, continues upward to an abandoned mine on the flank of Sheep Ridge. The road to the left at the intersection appears to be the route that descends into Sheep Park, but after a short and lovely jaunt it ends abruptly in an unmarked vehicle closure. The route to the right from the intersection, Forest Service Road 426, yields some lovely views of the high peaks of the Mosquito Range to the west.

Particularly on an early autumn morning, with the aspen in their full glory and with fresh snow on the mountains beyond, the Breakneck Pass area, especially at the crossroad junction, produces a magical experience of forested beauty. And it is an experience that the visitor can often savor alone, as few persons travel far into the Sheep Mountain area of Park County.

Because Browns Pass and Breakneck Pass are located in an area that once saw extensive mining activity, a variety of interesting side roads exist throughout the region. In addition to the Weston Pass road, the road to Mosquito Pass (*see* No. 6) begins just a few miles north of Fairplay. And about two miles north of the access road to Browns Pass, at a location just south of the US Highway 285-Colorado Highway 9 junction, a Forest Service access road along Fourmile Creek travels past the site of Horseshoe and, about three miles up the road, Leavick, a high mining camp built near timberline and named after prospector Felix Leavick. Once as large or larger then Horseshoe, Leavick included two large ore crushing mills and was the terminus of a three mile aerial tramway for the transportation of ore from the mines into town.

From the site of Leavick, the road continues upward to nearly thirteen thousand feet in elevation, with spurs leading to a variety of abandoned mining sites, principally the Lost Chance and Hill Top mines, located astride the flanks of Mount Sheridan and, to the south, Peerless Mountain. Because this road, much of it along the route of the Denver and South Park and Hilltop railroad, is relatively smooth and well maintained to Leavick, it offers two-wheel drive travelers uncommonly good backcountry access during fair-weather conditions.

A fall scene near the summit of Breakneck Pass.

54 La Salle Pass

Location: between Jefferson on US Highway 285 and Florissant on the east side of South Park

Difficulty: can be negotiated by some two-wheel drive vehicles under good conditions

Scenic Quality: excellent mountain vistas from the west side

Historic Interest: modest

Side Roads: several of considerable interest

High Point: 9,733 feet

Maps: USFS map of Pike National Forest at 1:125,000

USGS sheet 4 of Park County at 1:50,000

As the South Platte River flows out of South Park on its way to the eastern plains of Colorado, the river turns sharply from its southeasterly direction and heads northeast through Cheesman Reservoir and Chatfield Reservoir, then into Denver. The reason for this dramatic change of direction lies in the series of mountain ranges looming on the eastern edge of South Park: the Kenosha Mountains, the Tarryall Mountains, the Platte River Mountains and the Puma Hills.

The only paved road through these mountains is US 24 between Florissant and Hartsel, which crosses the Puma Hills at a 9,507 foot summit called Wilkerson Pass, along the abandoned route of the Colorado Midland railroad. A short distance to the north, another and far more obscure route travels through the Puma Hills between Martland Peak and Badger Peak, connecting the upper reaches of Tarryall Creek with the broad expanse of South Park. This route crosses the Puma Hills at a summit called La Salle Pass.

For visitors arriving from the Colorado Springs area, the easiest way to reach La Salle Pass is by way of US Highway 24, turning north on an improved gravel road (Park County Road 31) about four miles east of the Wilkerson Pass summit. The route to La Salle Pass is indicated by a sign about five miles up Park County Road 31 from US Highway 24. But far and away the most interesting and scenic route to La Salle Pass is to approach it from the north, by way of US Highway 285.

From US Highway 295 in South Park, several miles below Kenosha Pass, at the town of Jefferson, take Park County Road 77 southeast along

A view of the Sawatch Range and South Park from the west side of La Salle Pass.

Tarryall Creek, named for the gold mining camp established upstream from the highway in 1859. From this well-graded road above Tarryall Creek, travelers can enjoy views of the rock formations in the Platte River Mountains, the Kenosha Mountains and the Terryall Mountains to the north. The road follows an historic wagon route above Tarryall Creek to the mining camps of Tarryall and Hamilton, near the site of Como, once served by mule-pulled stagecoaches of the Central Overland California and Pikes Peak Express Company (of Pony Express fame). About sixteen miles from Jefferson, the road passes by small but scenic Tarryall Reservoir and continues through steeper countryside dotted with stands of pine. About 30 miles from Jefferson, Park County Road 31 diverges from Park County 77. Take Road 31 to the southwest at the site of Tarryall (which is not where the gold camp was located) and turn west several miles down the road at the sign pointing to La Salle Pass.

The relatively flat route traverses a meadow and crosses through a parcel of private land before climbing gently to the summit of La Salle Pass. At the summit, a sign points to an access road 4.5 miles in length to the summit of Badger Mountain (11,294 feet), where the Wilkerson fire lookout station is located. From the top of La Salle Pass the road rapidly breaks into open country-side, yielding a magnificent view of the Sawatch and Mosquito ranges rising above South Park. About one mile below the summit of the pass, however, a private land closure blocks ac-cess to US Highway 24 west of Wilkerson Pass. Travelers must therefore turn around and return to Park County Road 31.

In addition to the road from the summit of La Salle Pass to the top of Badger Mountain, there are a number of other interesting roads in the area. From US Highway 285 a mile east of Jefferson, the Lost Park Road winds up Long Gulch to the Lost Park Campground, near the entrance to the Lost Park Primitive Area, in a valley bordered by the Kenosha Mountains on one side and the Tarryall Mountains on the other side. Lost Park is reputedly the site where the last free-roaming bison in Colorado, three adults and a calf, were killed in 1897 and it is probably in commemoration of this sad event that the high mountain about three miles south of the Lost Park Campground is named Bison Peak.

From US Highway 24 about a mile east of Wilkerson Pass, a good quality side road drops down Caylor Gulch to Elevenmile Canyon Reservoir, a Denver Water Board reservoir fed by the South Fork of the South Platte River, and the Elevenmile State Recreation Area. From Lake George, on the east side of Wilkerson Pass by US Highway 24, additional improved gravel side roads wind down precipitous Elevenmile Canyon to the Reservoir and up Trail Creek to still other roads deep in Pike National Forest. As an additional sightseeing bonus, Florissant Fossil Beds National Monument is located just off US 24 a few miles east of Lake George.

Rock formations along Terryall Creek.

55 Ptarmigan Pass

Location: between Camp Hale on US Highway 24 and the Shrine Pass Road east of US Highway 24

Difficulty: four-wheel drive mandatory for the north side/see text note on special hazards

Scenic Quality: moderate

Historic Interest: modest except at south side base area, which is of high historic value

Side Roads: various in the area of scenic and historic interest

High Point: 11,777 feet

Maps: USFS map of White River National Forest at 1:125,000

USFS map of Arapaho National Forest (summit area only) at 1:125,000

USGS sheet 4 of Eagle County at 1:50,000

USGS sheet 2 of Summit County at 1:50,000

This little known pass route connects the upper Eagle River valley with the summit of the Gore Range in the area between Shrine Pass (*see* No. 20) and Fremont Pass; the route is named for Ptarmigan Hill, a 12,143 foot high peak directly west from the pass summit.

A more appropriate name for the pass might, however, be Camp Hale Pass, because the south side approach to the summit, by way of Resolution Creek, starts directly within the grounds of Camp Hale. This decommissioned U.S. Army training facility was established during World War II as the nation's sole location for mountain and winter warfare training. The 10th Mountain Division of the United States Army, which trained in this valley at Camp Hale, fought valiantly in Italian and Aleutian Island campaigns during the war. Afterward, a number of 10th Mountain veterans returned to Colorado to help found the state's downhill ski industry. A signboard beside Camp Hale on US Highway 24 provides background information on the area and two stone memorials at the summit of Tennessee Pass commemorate the achievements and losses this mountaineering division experienced.

The Ptarmigan Pass road is best approached from this south-side route through Camp Hale. From US Highway 24 turn in at the Camp Hale Recreation Area. From the north end of the site take Resolution Road (Forest Service Road 702) up a smooth, well-graded roadbed that climbs through wetlands and narrow valleys. The route

The deceptively smooth north side start of the road to Ptarmigan Pass.

then follows a slightly rougher shelf road that becomes a bit steeper as it approaches a timberline saddle crossing of the Gore Range with excellent views of the Sawatch Range to the west and the southwest. Under good road conditions, most backroad-capable smaller cars and light trucks can reach the summit from Camp Hale with limited difficulty.

At the pass summit, about five and one half miles from the base, a Forest Service sign warns of a rough road ahead. This cautionary note must not be taken lightly. For Ptarmigan Pass is a Jekyll and Hyde road, with a gentle southern side and a very rough, steep and demanding north side route along Forest Service Road 709 from the summit to its base on the Shrine Pass road, a bit less than three miles east of Redcliff. This north side approach—or descent, depending on your direction of travel—is not only steep and rough but very narrow, muddy, and laced with numerous stream crossings. Even as a route of descent it should be driven only by experienced and patient four-wheel drive operators with narrow track vehicles. Particularly at its lower elevations, this 5.7 miles road along Wearyman Creek is a scenic route, but not one for the faint of heart.

In addition to the sightseeing opportunities at Camp Hale, a number of other side trips are available in the Ptarmigan Pass area. From the south side of Camp Hale, a side road ascends the East Fork of the Eagle River to Robinson Lake and a privately owned crossing of the Gore Range into the mined waste disposal ponds from Amax's Climax molybdenum mine at the summit of Fremont Pass. A hiking trail from this East Fork road leads to the summit of Kokomo Pass, below which lies the abandoned mining town of Kokomo. From the very north end of Camp Hale, a rough four-wheel-drive route travels along McAllister Gulch and around Hornsilver Mountain to join the Ptarmigan Pass road a short distance above its junction with the Shrine Pass road.

Perhaps the most noteworthy of the side roads in the Ptarmigan Pass area is the well-traveled route up Homestake Creek to the Homestake Reservoir, created by the Fryingpan-Arkansas water diversion project high in the Sawatch Range. From US Highway 24 about midway between Redcliff and Camp Hale, a well-marked and well-maintained Forest Service Road at the Blodgett Campground ascends through the lovely countryside along Homestake Creek, terminating just above the dam (four-wheel drive is required for the final portion of this route) at the windswept and alpine setting of Homestake Reservoir.

Several miles below the reservoir, just beyond Gold Park Campground, a well-known and notorious side road winds and twists through the flanks of the Sawatch Range to the site of Holy Cross City and, beyond that former mining town, toward Hunky Dory Lake and Cleveland Lake. This route is well known because it provides the only motorized access into a large and highly scenic mountain area much of which is now designated as the Holy Cross Wilderness area. It is also notorious as one of the roughest and most difficult to negotiate four-wheel-drive roads in the Colorado Rockies; a punishing test of drivers and their vehicles. Having tried the road once myself, I decided it was not worth the mechanical wear and tear and turned back rather than risk the well-forged iron and stamped steel of an expensive vehicle on the cruel ruts and massive rocks that litter the way. My advice: park your vehicle at the base and start hiking unless motorized adventure—with perhaps a broken spring or bent axle—is on your agenda for the day.

10th Mountain Division memorial markers at the summit of Tennessee Pass, above Camp Hale.

56 Red Cone Pass

Location: between Webster on US Highway
  285 and Keystone on US Highway 40
Difficulty: four-wheel drive required/special
  caution mandatory on the west side
Scenic Quality: very high, with impressive
  summit views on both sides
Historic Interest: quite high
Side Roads: various routes of high scenic and
  historic interest are available
High Point: about 12,600 feet
Maps: USFS map of Arapaho National Forest
  at 1:125,000*
USFS map of Pike National Forest at
  1:125,000*
USGS sheet 2 of Summit County at 1:50,000*
USGS sheet 1 of Park County at 1:50,000*
*See special text note on maps of the area

    This little known pass route over the eastern
flank of Red Cone Peak, elevation 12,801 feet,
ranks among the highest pass roads in Colorado
and among the least known routes. Although the

roadway, such as it is, remains open to vehicular
traffic and is visible on the State's quadrangle
centered aerial photographs (Montezuma, No.
0654), map makers have often omitted the route
or shown it only as a pack trail veering off from
the more modern Webster Pass road (*see* No. 17).
Neither the USFS map of Arapaho National Forest nor the 1:50,000 County Map Series sheets
give any hint of this route. But it is shown as a
pack trail on the Montezuma fifteen minute Quadrangle map and as a separate crossing of the Continental Divide on the USFS map of Pike National
Forest.

    This alternative crossing from the South
Platte Valley into the ore-rich Snake River basin
is, however, a pass road in its own right and it is
related to Webster Pass in a manner not unlike
Engineer and Yvonne passes around Engineer
Mountain in the San Juan Mountains (*see* Nos. 46
& 47). The Webster Pass road and the Red Cone
Pass road will both take you from the same starting point to the same destination; it's just a ques-
tion of how you want to get there. The Webster
Pass road is a relatively mild, smooth route with

A roadside scene along the road to Red Cone Pass.

one long, narrow and demanding shelf road on the east side of the Continental Divide. Red Cone Pass, on the other hand, entails a long, hard and rough climb through the woods and along alpine meadows on the east side followed by a short but treacherously steep connecting link with the Webster Pass road just west of the past summit.

The road to Red Cone Pass—or call the route East Webster Pass, if you prefer, since it lacks an official name—starts on US Highway 285. Turn north on Park County Road 60 at the abandoned townsite of Webster and travel up the Webster Pass roadway about five miles. Just beyond the vicinity of the campground and picnic site, a side road to the right, sometimes marked by a sign, ascends through the woods along a rather rough, narrow and rocky route bordered by stands of aspen thinning to pine as the road climbs still higher, emerging to a long, jolting alpine traverse with excellent views to the north and to the west.

Near the summit of Red Cone Peak, the road climbs steeply in one final ascent to a narrow perch followed by an equally short and dangerously steep descent to the Webster Pass road near its summit. Experienced drivers of four-wheel-drive vehicles in excellent operating condition should encounter only minimal difficulty in making this sharp descent under dry road conditions, so long as they take their time about it. And after the rigors of the Red Cone Pass route, the drive down the west side of the Webster Pass road will seem like a relaxed and smooth journey. It may also be possible to drive east-bound up the sheer, rocky ascent to the summit of Red Cone Pass but I retain my doubts, having seen several vehicles try the road and lose traction well short of the top.

The many highly scenic and historically significant side roads in the area of Webster Pass are described in the Webster Pass section (*see* No. 17). These roads include the route up Peru Creek to the west side base of Argentine Pass (a magnificent high altitude journey), the short road up Deer Creek to a high mining site in a cirque on Rival Hill, visible from the summit of Webster and Red Cone passes, and the well-traveled but highly scenic road from Montezuma to Saints John (where passenger cars can go no further) and on to the Wild Irishman Mine, Swandyke and Breckenridge. Still other minor side roads on the west side of Red Cone Pass—and a few rough routes on the east side too—offer additional opportunities to explore deep into this historic mining region that once yielded such rich deposits of silver ore.

A view of Red Cone Peak from the Webster Pass road.

57 Gunsight Pass

Location: Ruby Range west of Crested Butte between the Slate River and Coal Creek
Difficulty: four-wheel drive required/long, narrow shelf road approach
Scenic Quality: beautiful scenic views/popular mountain bike route
Historic Interest: moderate
Side Roads: many of high scenic and historic interest
High Point: 12,090 feet
Maps: USFS map of Gunnison National Forest at 1:125,000 (does not show current route)
USGS sheet 2 of Gunnison County at 1:50,000

Colorado place names are often descriptive and sometimes repetitive. So it is with "gunsight pass." There are three such officially named passes in Colorado, all of them over twelve thousand feet high, all with summit elevations varying by less than 100 feet and two of the three are located in Gunnison National Forest a couple dozen miles from the City of Gunnison. The Gunsight Pass we are discussing here is the only such

pass, however, that is accessible by a road and open—if only on a most limited basis—to motor vehicles.

The western entrance to this high, dramatic crossing of an alpine ridge on the eastern flanks of the Ruby Range was by way of an access route from the Kebler Pass road (*see* Nos. 37 & 38) starting a few miles west of Crested Butte. For several years now this access point has been closed to the public by reason of a molybdenum mining venture in the vicinity of Mt. Emmons, just east of Gunsight Pass. Consequently, access to Gunsight Pass is now limited to a single route from the east, not shown as such on the USFS map of Gunnison National Forest, but marked by a sign at its start.

To find this route, travel north from Crested Butte on Colorado 135 toward Gothic, turning west on Gunnison County Road 734 at the first stop sign north of Crested Butte. Continue on this scenic road up the Slate River for about three miles, turning left at the Gunsight Pass road, marked also as Gunnison County Road 585. From this point beside a campground along the Slate River, the Gunsight Pass road winds steeply upward in a seemingly endless series of switchbacks

The view west into the Ruby Range from the road to Gunsight Pass.

that afford through the groves of roadside aspen a magnificent view of the Slate River Valley below and the Ruby Range to the west. The road remains quite smooth but becomes narrower, with occasional logs and boulders in the way, as it continues upward on a long shelf route to near timberline. Here the still distant but awesome summit of Gunsight Pass comes into view, looming as a shallow notch in a high alpine ridge, called Scarp Ridge, linking Mt. Emmons and Peeler Peak.

From this base point, below the site of the old Daisy Mine, the route ascends through a snowfield and often stays blocked through September. The route ascends a steeply carved valley onto a long, narrow and very exposed shelf road that tops the pass at a shallow summit notch. The road then descends steeply down to the Standard Mine and follows the Elk Creek Drainage to the Kebler Pass road.

Due to snow blockage, the final summit ascent to Gunsight Pass is usually closed to four-wheeled vehicles of any sort. Because of the relatively smooth and steep grades, this road to Gunsight Pass is a particularly challenging and appealing climb for mountain cyclists (of the human-powered type), who can often be seen pedaling up grades on this route that give pause even to vehicles equipped with large internal combustion engines. For visitors without access to pedal power, a hike of several miles is the usual route from the snowfield to the summit of Gunsight Pass.

Many of the side roads in the vicinity of Gunsight Pass are included in the sections of this book on Ohio and Kebler passes (Nos. 37 & 38) and the east side of Schofield Pass (No. 36). About one half mile up the Slate River road from the start of the Gunsight Pass route, a well-known side road for four-wheel-drive vehicles travels up Oh-be-joyful Creek deep into the Ruby Range, and from the end of the road hiking trails lead through Oh-be-joyful Pass (at 11,740 feet) and Daisy Pass (at 11,620 feet). Still another side road from the Slate River road follows a route up Poverty Gulch, in an area of extensive mining claims, nearly reaching the summit of Angel Pass. The Slate River road itself continues through the old mining town of Pittsburg to a mountain ridge crossing known locally as Paradise Divide and continues on to join the Schofield Pass road near its summit on the border of Pitkin and Gunnison counties.

A mountain cyclist below the high summit of Gunsight Pass.

58 Crooked Creek Pass

Location: between Eagle on I-70 and the Hagerman Pass Road

Difficulty: can be negotiated by smaller passenger cars and light trucks under good conditions

Scenic Quality: moderately high

Historic Interest: moderate with special interest along East Brush Creek

Side Roads: several of substantial interest

High Point: about 10,020 feet

Maps: USFS map of White River National Forest at 1:125,000

USGS sheet 3 of Eagle County at 1:50,000

USGS sheet 2 of Pitkin County at 1:50,000

This lovely and little-known pass route, higher and more obscure than West Cottonwood Pass, also traverses from the Interstate 70 corridor into the White River National Forest. In fact, a long, circuitous road connects the two pass routes. But the Crooked Creek Pass road, named for the minor drainage that descends from the south side of the summit, starts at the town of Eagle and ascends West Brush Creek to an open, gentle summit. From there it descends to the Hagerman Pass road (*see* No. 33) several miles above Ruedi Reservoir at Thomasville, an old-time railroad stop in the days when the Colorado Midland Railway traveled this route into the Roaring Fork valley.

Several scenic lakes border the Crooked Creek Pass route and on the north side of the route a well-traveled side road ascends East Brush Creek, a lovely tumbling stream bordered by wetlands. North of East Brush Creek is Adam Mountain, site of a proposed and controversial downhill ski area called Adam's Rib (named for a prominent ridge on Adam Mountain). And behind Adam Mountain is a taller (by eleven feet) and some say more shapely peak called Mt. Eve. Farther up the Brush Creek route, on a tributary drainage about ten miles from the confluence with East Brush

The confluence of East and West Brush creeks on the way to Crooked Creek Pass.

Creek, lies the townsite of Fulford, an abandoned mining community below 12,550-foot-high New York Peak. Several Forest Service campgrounds are available in the area, and the Fulford Cave is located at the end of a short hiking trail that begins at the Fulford Cave Campground.

To reach Crooked Creek Pass from the north, take the Eagle exit on Interstate 70 and travel south on Capital Street, following a windy and somewhat roughly paved road through a wide ranching valley that begins to narrow and then branches at the pavement's end, where East Brush Creek flows into the west fork of the same creek. From this confluence it is a ten mile trip up East Brush Creek to Fulford, about four miles up West Brush Creek to Sylvan Lake, and an additional twenty-six miles from Sylvan Lake to Ruedi Reservoir on the Hagerman Pass road. The road to Sylvan Lake is well maintained and heavily traveled in the summertime. From Sylvan Lake a somewhat narrower and rougher road beside an unsightly powerline corridor travels over the gentle, open ridge of Crooked Creek Pass. The road then continues through Crooked Creek Park, beside Crooked Creek Reservoir, through Lime Park and then it descends with several sharp turns and switchbacks to the Thomasville townsite on the Hagerman Pass road.

Several miles south of the pass summit a side road on the east leads to Woods Lake, located on private property, and this route, just to the west of Burnt Mountain, also leads south across the Pitkin County border to the Hagerman Pass road four miles above Thomasville. Once on the Hagerman Pass road, travelers can elect to continue up the route past Ivanhoe Lake to the Hagerman Pass summit (a sturdy truck and/or four-wheel drive is usually required for the rough summit climb) and down to Leadville. Or you can travel south on the smoothly paved route to lovely Ruedi Reservoir and the town of Basalt on Colorado 82, where the Fryingpan River empties into the Roaring Fork. From this point it is a short highway trip down Colorado 82 to Glenwood Springs and I-70 or a much longer but splendidly scenic trip east on Colorado 82 to Aspen and over Independence Pass to US Highway 24.

In addition to the side roads already mentioned, most notably the route up East Brush Creek (a portion of which is quite rough and can require four-wheel drive) to Fulford, other roads, again mostly for backcountry-capable vehicles only, diverge from the Crooked Creek Pass road. These routes, located near Sylvan Lake and the pass summit, travel back into Hardscrabble

Mountain, along Gypsum Creek and along East Brush Creek by Fulford. Even without getting lost, there are enough roads on the north side of Crooked Creek Pass to keep most travelers well occupied for a day of sightseeing in this one corner of White River National Forest.

An early winter view up West Brush Creek.

59 West Cottonwood Pass

Location: between Gypsum on I-70 and
   Carbondale on Colorado Highway 82
Difficulty: can be negotiated by smaller
   passenger cars under good conditions—but
   beware mud
Scenic Quality: best views southbound on
   south side
Historic Interest: moderate
Side Roads: a variety on both sides of the
   summit
High Point: 8,280 feet
Maps: USFS map of White River National
   Forest at 1:125,000
USGS sheet 3 of Eagle County at 1:50,000
USGS sheet 5 of Garfield County at 1:50,000

This other Cottonwood Pass (*see* also No. 32) is lower, less spectacular and less well known than its namesake crossing of the Continental Divide through the Sawatch Range between the Upper Arkansas Valley and Taylor Park. But it is a convenient, attractive and well established route between the Aspen area and I-70 to the north. And,

as an extra bonus, it offers to southbound travelers on its south side, a stunning view of Snowmass Mountain and the other high peaks of the Elk Range located in the Maroon Bells-Snowmass Wilderness.

Because of its low elevation—almost the entire route is below eight thousand feet—the Cottonwood-Carbondale road remains open during a longer season than any other backcountry pass road in the vicinity. Except during periods of significant snow accumulation, the major hazard on the road is occasionally deep mud on the north side of the summit. Vehicles without four-wheel drive should turn back rather than risk getting trapped in the deep ruts and slippery surface that sometimes develops at lower elevations on the I-70 side of the pass. In addition, drivers should remain on the lookout for large trucks pulling horse trailers around the curves on both sides of the pass summit.

For north bound travelers, the approach to West Cottonwood Pass starts at Exit 140 on Interstate 70 at the town of Gypsum. From the edge of town, travel south on the paved highway to Valley Road, go right about 1.5 miles to the

The view south from below the summit of West Cottonwood Pass.

Cottonwood Pass sign, and there turn west on Eagle County Road 10A. The route to the pass follows a sweeping dirt road through a broad valley, then climbs through piñon-juniper scrub country before dropping very steeply along a one lane road to a narrow valley. The road then begins climbing again beside stands of aspen and scrub oak to a broad plateau crest dotted with ponds and subdivided lots for sale to any eager flatlander.

From this gentle summit, the route begins an easy descent through open ranching valleys with majestic views of Capital Peak, Snowmass Mountain (both fourteeners) Mt. Sopris and other high Elk Range peaks. From the lower portion of the road, a variety of exit routes spread downhill along Cattle Creek, Crystal Creek, Blue Creek and other drainages to Colorado 82 in the Carbondale area. From these termination points it is a short journey downstream to Glenwood Springs or up the Roaring Fork Valley to Snowmass and Aspen. Alternately, intrepid pass route travelers can either proceed up the Fryingpan River at Basalt and take Crooked Creek Pass (*see* No. 58) back to I-70 at the town of Eagle or continue up the Fryingpan to the summit of Hagerman Pass (*see* No. 33) and down to Leadville.

A variety of side roads lead off from the West Cottonwood main route. At the town of Gypsum, an alternate paved route, turning to a graveled surface, travels up Gypsum Creek to the Crooked Creek Pass road above Sylvan lakes. Another side road from near the summit of the pass traverses a long route along Red Table Mountain with hiking trail access to rarely visited Taylor Creek Pass.

Unlike the majority of backcountry pass roads in Colorado, nearly the entire length of the West Cottonwood Pass route travels through private property or Bureau of Land Management (BLM) lands leased for livestock grazing. So travelers along the road should take caution not to trespass and recognize that a number of the scenic side routes are also located on privately owned or leased land not open to public travel.

60 Columbine Pass

Location: between Delta on US Highway 50 and Nucla near Colorado Highway 141

Difficulty: can be negotiated by two-wheel drive vehicles under good summer and fall conditions but beware mud and large trucks

Scenic Quality: lovely with especially good west side views

Historic Interest: modest

Side Roads: numerous alternate routes and local side roads

High Point: 9,120 feet

Maps: USFS map of Uncompahgre National Forest at 1:125,000

USGS sheet 1 of Montrose County at 1:50,000

Between the Uncompahgre River, flowing northwest through Ouray, and the San Miguel River, which originates high in the San Juan Mountains above Telluride, there lies a long, relatively low plateau of gentle forest lands blessed with streams and small lakes. Called the Uncompahgre Plateau, this land was long a seasonal hunting preserve of the Ute Indians, who roamed the valleys and mountains of western Colorado for centuries.

Henry Gannett, a topographer with the Hayden Survey, visited the Uncompahgre Plateau in 1874 and wrote of it:

In the interior, near the crest, the land is, to the Utes, one flowing with milk and honey. Here are fine streams of cold water, beautiful aspen groves, the best of grasses in the greatest abundance, and a profusion of wild fruit and berries, while the country is a perfect flower garden.

Except for the periodic logging operations, some cattle grazing, a few abandoned uranium mines, and a network of dirt roads, not much has changed on the Uncompahgre Plateau in more than a century. Wildlife still glide through the moist forests sprinkled with wildflowers and the clear skies above normally yield to afternoon thundershowers in the summertime and fall.

A single long route, called the Divide Road, more than sixty miles in length, traverses the

A crossroads near the summit of Columbine Pass.

crest of the plateau, peaking at a crossing called Columbine Pass. And another back road, this one from Montrose, in the Uncompahgre Valley, also travels over Columbine Pass on the route to Nucla and Uravan, small communities below the western edge of the plateau. Indeed, if there is a single central crossroads on the Uncompahgre Plateau, toward which nearly all roads lead, it is by the summit of Columbine Pass.

Travelers wishing to journey along the Uncompahgre Plateau by way of Columbine Pass have available a wide variety of routes; they can start or end their journey in Grand Junction, Delta, Montrose or Nucla. The route I most enjoy, however, starts in Delta on US Highway 50. Turn west from the highway on 6th Street (Colorado Highway 348) in Delta and continue west on the US Forest Service Delta-Nucla access road where Colorado 348 bears south at the Church of the First Born. This route along Cottonwood Creek climbs from the Uncompahgre River through dry, rolling hills of piñon and juniper to the rim of a dramatic canyon, where Monitor Creek flows. Then it descends into a lovely valley, with delightful views, especially in the fall, when the roadside scrub oak is ablaze with color. The gentle route to the summit continues through stands of mature aspen mixed with pine to a low crossing about thirty-five miles from Delta.

At the summit, a road to the right (that is, the north) leads along the west side of the plateau with sweeping views of the magnificent Tabeguache Basin, bitterly defended by the Ute Indians from encroaching whites, and further beyond, the Sneffels Range. Lone Cone Peak and the La Plata Mountains rise in the background. This route then winds down Coal Canyon to Road 2900 and west on Road DD to Colorado Highway 97 a short distance outside the town of Nucla. From the summit of Columbine Pass a road to the left (this is, the south), the Divide Road again, travels down to Montrose or, alternatively, on a side road, back down to Colorado 145. About one mile east of Columbine Pass summit, at a road junction, another route leads northwest on the Divide Road for travelers wishing to take the long trip down to Colorado Highway 141 near its junction with US 50 at the town of Whitewater.

My favorite choice, however, is to skip these alternate roads and travel directly down the

The hanging flume (lower right and center) in Unaweep Canyon.

Distant San Juan peaks seen from the southern edge of the Uncompahgre Plateau.

plateau to Nucla, enjoying the mountain views along the way. From Nucla (established as a utopian community about 1890 by the Colorado Cooperative Company) and the short trip down Colorado 97 to Colorado 141 at Naturita, travelers are faced with a pleasant choice indeed. By going eastbound (actually southeast), they will journey along scenic Colorado 145 with an opportunity to stop at Telluride or to take Colorado 62 at Placerville over the spectacular Dallas Divide road, with majestic close-up views of the Sneffels Range to the south as they approach the town of Ridgeway. From Ridgeway, US Highway 550 leads south through Ouray over Red Mountain Pass or north on US 550 to Montrose, Delta and Grand Junction.

The other choice available to visitors in Nucla or Naturita is to travel Colorado 141 northwest up the scenic river valley through Uravan (named for the twin elements or uranium and vanadium found in the area) and Gateway. This magnificent road, little-known by most east-slope Coloradans, traverses the steep and spectacular canyon of the San Miguel River, which joins the Dolores River. A portion of the famous hanging flume is visible from the road.

This long wood waterway, precariously driven into the canyon walls, was once known as the Colorado Cooperative Ditch and was constructed to bring water from the upper reaches of the San Miguel River to First Park Mesa, a farming area near Nucla. Beyond the canyon, Colorado Highway 141 travels through scenic countryside alongside the Dolores River to Gateway, where the road continues its lovely route through still more scenic landscapes just below the northern edge of the Uncompahgre Plateau, before ending at US Highway 50 a short distance south of Grand Junction.

In addition to this abundance of major backroads in the area, there are many more side roads throughout the Uncompahgre Plateau itself. Various maps of the area show many but not all of these routes, which are often used on a temporary basis for logging operations. Visitors to the area will find that these routes offer convenient access deep into the plateau. But all such side roads, and often the main roads too, should be approached with great caution. Even during dry warm weather in the valley below, the roads of the Uncompahgre plateau often become thick rivers of mud.

Under these conditions, as my friend Glenn has told me, nothing short of a tracked vehicle, not even front and rear chains on a four-wheel-drive vehicle, will guarantee you passage through the thick mud. Doubting him once on this matter, I tried negotiating a side road during a rainy period and was rescued from the mud several hours later with the aid of a long, long tow chain and a Forest Service truck.

61 Baxter Pass

Location: between Interstate 70 west of Grand Junction and Bonanza, Utah at the terminus of Utah Highway 45
Difficulty: suitable for many two-wheel drive vehicles under dry conditions
Scenic Quality: moderate
Historic Interest: slight
Side Roads: various of interest/see text note on private land closures
High Point: 8,422 feet
Maps: USGS sheet 2 of Garfield County at 1:50,000

Baxter Pass may not be the highest, the most scenic or the most historically important of Colorado's backroad passes, but it is probably the most remote of such officially recognized routes, a collector's item for those of us who take special pride in knowing and having been to off-the-beaten-track places where few else have troubled to venture. The road starts next to nowhere and ends many miles later in an even more obscure location, but in between there are sights and experiences to make the journey worthwhile.

Normally, travelers journeying north from the Grand Valley area around Grand Junction take Colorado 139, the Douglas Pass (elevation 8,268 feet) route, to Rangely and points beyond. This pass road, the summit of which is named for a Ute Indian chief who helped lead the Ute uprising at the White River Agency near Meeker in 1879, is a paved all-weather route through a vast expanse of little-visited plateau countryside along the western edge of Colorado. Though occasionally prone to earth slides, the road is a pleasant enough drive north from the town of Loma, with sweeping views of the canyon country and sagebrush-juniper flats of western Rio Blanco and Garfield counties.

Baxter Pass, the lesser known twin of Douglas Pass, is only slightly higher in elevation and traverses similar landscape, but it affords

The "8 Road" access to Baxter Pass from the town of Mack.

visitors an opportunity to move at a more leisurely pace and to explore in detail a portion of Colorado not often visited by most travelers. In fact, simply locating the road to Baxter Pass can prove to be a bit of an adventure, as even local residents seem a bit confused about its location.

From Interstate 70, take Exit 11 to the Town of Mack, a community that was once a shipping point for sheep and the eastern terminus of the narrow-gauge Uintah Railroad. Turn left at the stop sign (there is only one stop sign in Mack) and travel west along the old highway for about two and one-half miles to 8 Road, where a roadside sign points the way to Baxter Pass. Turn north, continue to S Road, and turn west. Follow S Road until the pavement ends and the route becomes a graveled road that turns sharply to the north and travels through a barren sage plateau covered with low, rolling hills and cliffs looming in the distance. Deeper into this vast, desolate landscape, the road passes by a variety of natural gas wells, pumps, compressors and other fixtures amid high, sculpted cliffs of sandstone.

The route continues up West Salt Creek into a wide canyon that begins to narrow. Then the road swings to the left into Railroad Canyon and climbs to the summit of Baxter Pass in a series of switchbacks. From the top of the pass, the road descends through West Evacuation Creek and past McAndrews Lake; at that point the traveler

is about 60 miles from Rangely and perhaps 30 miles from Bonanza, Utah. During good weather conditions, the road is navigable by most two-wheel-drive vehicles but occasional rainy periods produce deep mud holes and long mud slides where even four-wheel vehicles are at risk of becoming mired in the deep muck.

The Baxter Pass road is intersected by many side roads. On the lower portion of the route and also from the summit of the pass many of these roads lead to remote gas wells, dry holes and pumping equipment scattered throughout the Garmesa (derived from Garfield and Mesa counties) Natural Gas Fields. About one mile beyond the Railroad Creek turnoff to Baxter Pass, twin side roads continue up the East Branch and the West Branch of West Salt Creek.

From the west side of the summit of Baxter Pass, additional side roads branch off to Rat Hole Ridge, Atchee Ridge and Lone Spring Ridge before disappearing into the vast, dry and desolate plateau lands of eastern Utah. Travelers wishing to explore these routes should proceed with caution, however. Nearly all of this countryside is in private ownership (the Baxter Pass area lies far from any Forest Service lands) and many of the roads are closed to public travel. The area is sufficiently remote that one could be lost or stranded for days before assistance arrived.

A gas field facility on the road to Baxter Pass.

62 No Name Pass

Location: between Cuchara on Colorado
  Highway 12 and the San Luis Valley
Difficulty: two-wheel drive accessible from the
  west with permission required/single track
  vehicles or horseback required from the
  east
Scenic Quality: moderate
Historic Interest: negligible
Side Roads: several available in the area
High Point: 10,100 feet
Maps: USFS map of San Isabel National
  Forest at 1:125,000
USGS sheet 4 of Huerfano County at 1:50,000
USGS sheet 2 of Costilla County at 1:50,000

There does not exist any pass route in Colorado officially called "No Name Pass." But there
are so many informal mountain crossings in Colorado which the United States Board on Geographic Names has never named and which are
not even known locally by a commonly accepted

name that I think it appropriate to include one
such route as representative of the many. It is
not a pass route especially remarkable for its
historic interest, the scenery along the way, or
any other particular feature. But it is certainly a
pleasant enough route along the forested flanks
of the Sangre de Cristos and one that well
represents the enjoyment of exploring the Colorado backcountry.

In fact, the purpose of my journey into the
Sangre de Cristo Range that day was not to find
new passes at all, but to scout for elk in the company of several friends who also wished to explore
a route one of us had heard about but none had
visited. That we happened upon a little-known
mountain crossing simply added to the enjoyment of the day.

How does one find No Name Pass, or at least
this no name pass? Take US Highway 160 to La
Veta (west of Walsenburg) and then follow the
lovely winding route of Colorado Highway 12
south through the town of Cuchara. About three
miles up the road toward Cucharas Pass turn west

Route finding on the way to No Name Pass.

on the good quality graveled Forest Service road to Blue Lake and Bear Lake. At the west end of the Bear Lake Campground, a Forest Service sign points toward a wide trail open to motorcycles and narrow track three and four wheel recreational vehicles, but too narrow for full-size motor vehicles.

The route, known as Indian Trail and shown on the Forest Service map as a hiking trail, winds, twists and squirms its way up hills and down gullies on a course parallel with the Sangre de Cristo Range. After about a half dozen miles of wandering through a dense forest of pine and aspen, the route descends gently (if you do not get lost in the maze of side roads branching off deeper into the forest) to the smooth meadowlands of Bonnett Park, about one mile southeast of Harrison Peak. The route continues through Bonnett Park, again enters a wooded glade and ends at a nearly level and forested crossing point of the Sangre de Cristos marked by a barbed wire fence.

Beyond the fence, on the west side of the summit, lies a smoothly graded road and the vast expanse of the former Trinchera Grant, a Spanish land grant from the age of the Conquistadors that has passed into eastern ownership principally for second home subdivision development. The west side route from No Name Pass travels down West Indian Creek and, by way of several roads, through McCarty Park and on to the main road leading to the Forbes Trinchera development from US Highway 160 east of Fort Garland and from Colorado 159 between Fort Garland and San Luis. Access to the west side of this route is on privately owned land but is reportedly available by registration at the Trinchera ranch office and payment of a nominal daily user fee.

Our efforts to navigate the network of roads leading into Bonnett Park were aided by a knowledgable local pathfinder and backcountry traveling companion, Andrew Nigrini. In the absence of his services, I urge that visitors to the area rely on the USGS 7.5 minute topographic map of the area (McCarty Park) rather than the USFS map of San Isabel National Forest, which provides only limited assistance.

In addition to No Name Pass, this particularly scenic corner of Colorado also includes La Veta Pass (*see* No. 14), Apishapa Pass (*see* No. 15), Whiskey Pass (a high Sangre de Cristo crossing on private land within the old Maxwell Grant) and still another unnamed pass road from the town of La Veta up Indian Creek and down into McCarty Park on the west slope of the Sangre de Cristos.

This land is not for you and me. A private closure north of the Spanish Peaks.

A peaceful summer scene in Grand Mesa National Forest.

A Sampler Of Additional Pass Roads

Are the various pass roads featured—or at least mentioned—in this book the total of such roads in Colorado? They certainly include nearly all the high pass roads in the state that carry officially sanctioned names and many of the lesser routes as well. But I continue to learn of new pass roads from my own travels, from conversations with friends and from reader correspondence. If indeed I had traveled all these new roads too, my heart would be a bit heavy knowing that there were no more such routes to attempt. Instead, I remain encouraged that next season there will always be still more roads to travel; more places to visit. Presented below is a sampling of six additional roads to travel:

Bolam Pass

North of Durango, in the San Juan National Forest, nearly all the roads, such as US Highway 550 and Colorado 145, run in a north-south direction, following the course of the Animas and Dolores rivers and their tributaries. In the rugged countryside, between peaks along the border of Montezuma County and La Plata County, is Bolam Pass, an officially designated crossing about 11,180 feet high, that provides a link through this countryside, connecting the two major river valleys.

Starting about six miles north of Rico, at the Clayton Campground, a good quality road, that soon deteriorates as it climbs above Barlow Creek, travels across the divide at Bolam Pass and appears to still connect with a roadway link from the Graysill Mine down Hermosa Creek to US Highway 550 a short distance north of the Purgatory Ski Area.

Scotch Creek Pass

Still another pass route, several miles to the south of Bolam Pass, connects the same two river valleys. This other crossing point, also in the San Juan National Forest, is not named, but with a summit elevation of about 10,400 feet, it offers a lower crossing than its higher and more dramatic neighbor to the north.

Where is Scotch Creek Pass? Starting about three miles south of Rico on Colorado Highway 145, a rough four-wheel drive road to the east parallels Scotch Creek, appearing to cross over the same ridge line as Bolam Pass but at a lower point. The route then follows Hotel Draw to an improved road along the East Fork of Hermosa Creek and US Highway 550 just beyond the Purgatory Ski Area.

Kennebec Pass

About a dozen miles south of Scotch Creek Pass, high in the La Plata Mountains above the town of La Plata, lies an arc of once rich gold and silver mines that first opened in the mid 1870s and have been worked periodically into the 1950s. Kennebec Pass provides a linkage north of Snowstorm Peak among these mining claims. To reach Kennebec Pass, take US Highway 160 west from Durango to a short distance beyond Hesperus—a coal mining town and supply camp for the mines to the north—and turn north on the paved road to Mayday and La Plata. Then continue north up the La Plata River along a four-wheel-drive road that climbs through this extensive mining district to Kennebec Pass, an above-timberline crossing on the north side of 12,388-foot Cumberland Mountain. From the pass, a route several miles long, which may no longer be navigable to motor vehicles, crosses to a relatively smooth Forest Service road that winds and twists its way to Junction Creek and continues along a paved surface into the City of Durango.

Side roads along this route lead off to a number of the larger mines in the district, including the Jennie Lind Mine, the Columbus Mine and the Neglected Mine. The road about one mile north of La Plata that follows the course of Lewis Creek to the old Jennie Lind and Western Belle mines is also an old pass road, over 11,776-foot Eagle Pass, along a route that connects a number of now-abandoned mining camps and claims.

Lone Cone passes

Still in this same portion of San Juan National Forest is yet another pass road, unnamed but better maintained and graded than the three previous routes. It crosses into the San Juan National Forest from the Uncompahgre National Forest at a low point about 8,600 feet in elevation on the west side of the Wilson Mountains between Dunn Peak and Groundhog Peak and provides access to a broad expanse of mountain terrain along the West Dolores River.

The easiest way to reach Lone Cone Pass is from Colorado 145, west of the Dallas Divide, at the town of Norwood, where a large sign points to the Lone Cone Forest Service access road. Take this good quality road directly south, bearing to the east beyond Cone Reservoir. The road is well-maintained to the Lone Cone Forest Service Station and Beaver Peak and continues climbing, more steeply, from there to the pass summit. At a point below the summit, the road divides. The route to the southwest goes to Groundhog Reservoir, Miramonte State Recreation Area and beyond, while the route to the southeast follows a winding course to Dunton, once a small mining town, and then parallels the West Dolores River all the way to its confluence with the main branch of the Dolores River at Colorado Highway 145 north of the City of Cortez.

As an additional bonus, this long route past the Wilson Mountains offers an unusually wide variety of additional roads to explore on both sides of the pass, some suitable for two-wheel and some only for four-wheel-drive vehicles. In addition, a rough side road indicated on the Forest Service map of San Juan National Forest as a four-wheel-drive route, provides another, higher pass road crossing at about 10,700 feet (which perhaps should be called East Lone Cone Pass) of the same ridge that Lone Cone Pass traverses.

Carson Pass

The original town of Carson, one of the most remote mining camps in Colorado, enjoyed the unique distinction of sitting directly astride the Continental Divide. Named after Chris Carson, a prospector who found gold or silver ore in the area, Carson was founded in the early 1880s and not deserted until the early years of this century. Many of the mining structures and cabins around Carson have since vanished, but enough remains to qualify it as a bona fide ghost town.

With the construction of a wagon road along Lost Trail Creek in 1897, Carson Pass stood at the top of a road connecting Lake City and the Lake Fork of the Gunnison River with the upper Rio Grande River Valley above Creede. But the south side of the route has deteriorated to the point where it is not reportedly open to motor vehicles, and the only motorized access to Carson Pass and the Carson townsite is from the north. To reach Carson Pass, take Colorado Highway 149 south from Lake City and continue on the smoothly graveled road south to Lake San Cristobal and the Williams Creek Campground. About two miles

beyond the campground, a rough four-wheel-drive road travels up Wager Gulch and past the Carson townsite to Carson Pass (at about 12,350 feet), a slow journey of some four or five miles.

No major side roads diverge from the Carson Pass route. But the road along the Lake Fork of the Gunnison River, past Lake San Cristobal, is the eastside access road to magnificent Cinnamon Pass (see No. 45) and the main road west from Lake City travels to American Flats and over the Engineer Mountain Passes (see Nos. 46, 47).

Hightower Mountain passes

This set of two pass roads, one little-known and the other utterly obscure, was suggested to me (along with an impressive number of other remote pass roads) by Will Davis, an insatiable traveler of Colorado's backcountry pass routes. Indeed, I had once traveled one of these two routes without even recognizing it as a pass road until Will pointed it out to me. Indeed, no official name exists for either of these two crossings from the far northeast corner of Grand Mesa National Forest into the White River National Forest. Nor, indeed, do these two routes have much in common, except that they they both start from the west on Buzzard Creek and travel around opposite sides of Hightower Mountain into a remote portion of White River National Forest.

West Hightower Mountain Pass, if we may call it that, is the more readily traveled of the two roads and it provides a scenic, if slow, backcountry link between the Interstate 70 communities of Grand Junction and Silt. To reach West Hightower Mountain Pass from Grand Junction, take Interstate 70 east to Colorado Highway 65 and follow the winding course of Plateau Creek, then continue east on Colorado Highway 330 through Colbran. About six miles to the east, exit on a good quality gravel road that gently ascends the Buzzard Creek drainage, and is suitable for most two-wheel-drive vehicles under favorable conditions.

From this junction, the road gently climbs through privately owned grazing lands, and branches up Road Creek into Grand Mesa National Forest. Several miles later it ascends a slow rise (the pass summit) through open meadows and then drops a bit more steeply through several miles in White River National Forest. The route continues north along a maze of graveled roads, most all of which ultimately terminate near the town of Silt, a quiet community on Interstate Highway 70 between Rifle and Glenwood Springs.

Starting from the west, the road to East Hightower Mountain Pass also begins on Colorado Highway 65 from Interstate 70 east of Grand Junction. The route continues along Colorado 330 through Colbrand and exits the paved road to ascend along Buzzard Creek. But rather than branching north along Road Gulch, this route continues southeast along Buzzard Creek to a less well-traveled road at Owens Creek, ascending through the countryside in the most easterly tip of Grand Mesa National Forest. About a mile from the boundary of White River National Forest, a rough side road to the north (left) crosses a nearby divide and then it descends by a four-wheel-drive route along West Williams Creek to a road juncture several miles below the pass summit. The roads to the left lead through a complex maze of routes west around Baldy Mountain and north to Interstate 70 in the vicinity of Silt. The roads to the right lead east around Baldy Mountain and Haystack Gate to a good quality Forest Service road that eventually winds out of White River National Forest and past the Glenwood Springs airport to Colorado Highway 82 just south of Glenwood Springs and Interstate Highway 70.

If these routes to and from the two Hightower Mountain passes seem a bit confusing, they are, simply because the countryside is interlaced with such a variety of roads. The opportunities to get lost are many, but so too is the opportunity to explore the back roads of Colorado equally great. My advice? Take along plenty of gasoline, the proper maps and enjoy the trip.

Appendix A
A Note on Maps and Route Finding

Travelers have used maps for centuries to guide their way through the Rocky Mountains. In recent years, however, the traditional cartographic techniques of field surveying coupled with a bit—and sometimes more—of guestimation have given way to stereoscopic aerial photography and automated plotting backed up by occasional field checks. The resulting maps, though not perfect, display vast amounts of information with a greater degree of accuracy than most recreational travelers will ever need.

For foot-powered travel, the preferred map series is usually the United States Geologic Survey (USGS) 7.5-minute topographic maps, produced at a scale of 1:24,000 (1 inch = 2,000 feet). These maps, although they provide excellent detail, cover only a limited amount of terrain. In addition, some of the 7.5-minute quadrangle maps, along with many of the 15-minute, 1:62,500 scale (1 inch = 1 mile) topographic maps, are outdated; a few have undergone no significant revision in more than one-half century.

For motorized travel in the mountains, the 7.5-minute topographic maps are useful primarily when exploring a selected area in detail or when searching for a small site not shown on other maps. But to cover the area that can be traversed in a full day of vehicle travel could require nearly a briefcase full of the 7.5-minute maps. A superior series of maps for motorized travel in Colorado is the new county map series, produced at a scale of 1:50,000 (1 inch = about 4,000 feet). Not only do these maps show contour lines, a characteristic of topographic maps, but they benefit from revisions based on recent aerial photography. The large sheet format allows each map to cover a substantial amount of terrain, often six or eight times the area of the older 7.5-minute maps. Yet, the 1:50,000 scale provides ample detail for nearly all recreational uses. The appropriate county map series sheets are listed at the heading of each pass description. These sheets and the USGS 7.5-minute and 15-minute maps can be purchased at various local retail outlets or directly from the government at the Federal Center and the Federal Office Building in Denver, Colorado.

Neither of the map series discussed so far provides an overview of an entire mountain range or drainage basin. This function is best served by the U.S. Forest Service maps at a 1:125,000 scale (1 inch = 2 miles) for each of the national forests in Colorado. The Forest Service map series does not include contour lines, but it displays nearly all major backcountry roads, many of the minor roads, and many of the hiking trails that traverse Forest Service lands. Nearly all the backcountry pass roads discussed in this book are shown on the Forest Service map series, although some of them are not named. The appropriate Forest Service maps appear at the heading of each pass description. Individual national forest maps can be purchased from local Forest Service offices, and complete map sets may still be available on a limited basis from the National Forest Service regional office in Denver. High-quality maps of Colorado depicting the state's highway network and all National Forests are distributed without charge by the Colorado Division of Commerce and Development and the Colorado Department of Highways.

Even the best maps, however, are of little use without the knowledge and equipment to use them effectively for route finding and the identification of local features. Basic map reading skills can be acquired readily from several hours spent studying one of the many good publications on this subject. The equipment needed to make effective use of maps in the field includes a compass (preferably the type that allows a user to take bearings), a ruler, and a dial-type distance-measuring instrument to calculate the length of curved lines. With this elementary equipment, a bit of practice, the appropriate maps, and a convenient way to store them, backcountry travel becomes a safer, simpler, and more enjoyable experience.

Appendix B
Proper Equipment

The field research necessary to complete this book required some 12,000 miles of travel by various passenger cars, four jeeps, and two motorcycles over some of the worst roads in Colorado and under occasionally poor weather conditions. Fortunately, I never suffered bodily harm, injured no one, seriously damaged no motor vehicles, got stuck only once, and never failed to get home eventually under my own power. Plain good luck certainly helped. So, too, did my reluctance to take more than a minimum of risks. But proper equipment also played an important role along with prior planning.

Proper equipment is not necessarily a matter of major cash outlays. It is a matter of ensuring that the equipment on which you will rely is in good working order, that it is appropriate to the tasks at hand, and that you understand how to use it. For foot-powered travelers, the task of deciding what to bring is simplified because carrying capacity is sorely limited and one need care only for one's self and not also for a complex piece of machinery.

Motor vehicle travelers should also be prepared to use their feet for walking. Hopefully by design and sometimes by accident they, too, will find themselves foot-powered. Accordingly, the additional carrying capacity that a vehicle affords should be used in anticipation of this possibility.

You therefore should carry into the backcountry an appropriate selection of personal gear and vehicular equipment. Let's look first at personal gear. The Colorado Mountain Club, which is an organization with better than one-half century of experience promoting preparedness for mountain travel, requires its prospective members to learn the ten essentials that must always accompany them into the mountains. These ten essentials are:

- maps—of the area
- compass—and the ability to use it
- flashlight—with a spare bulb and batteries
- sunglasses—of good optical quality
- matches—wooden, waterproofed, and with a candle
- pocketknife—with multiple-purpose blades
- extra food—nuts, dried fruit, and hard candy recommended
- extra clothing—including a hat, gloves, and heavy jacket

- first aid kit—and a small container to store it in
- survival kit—whistle, mirror, nylon cord, etc.

To this list I would add a large mouth canteen filled with water, a cotton bandana, a pencil, spare eyeglasses for those who need them, and a sturdy pack in which to carry all these items.

Assembling this list of sundries prior to every trip requires patience and prior planning. Consequently, you should keep a set of these items already collected together in a pack and ready to go into your vehicle. Better yet, store the pack in the vehicle so that it will always be available when needed.

What about the proper equipment for motorized backcountry travel? Here are ten essentials in addition to the items already listed:

- shovel—with a long handle
- tow cable—the longer and stronger the better
- heavy-duty jack—rated at more than 50 percent of vehicle weight
- flares—preferably the spiked bottom type
- extra blankets—or a spare sleeping bag
- gas can and siphon—for lending, borrowing, or transferring fluids
- fire extinguisher—of a type rated for electrical and gasoline fires
- spare parts—including a fan belt, fuses, ignition points, etc.
- tool kit—including a repair manual, screwdrivers, wrenches, vise grip pliers, tire gauge, circuit tester, etc.
- emergency kit—including chains, elastic bungee stretch cords, compressed tire sealer and/or portable air tank, repair tape, etc.

Serious backcountry and off-road travel enthusiasts would consider this list only a partial description of what is needed. But with a little bit of ingenuity, these essentials can serve a wide variety of purposes. A spare gasoline can not only augments the cruising range of a vehicle, it also represents an independent supply in the event of a punctured tank and can be used for such purposes as hauling water from a stream to replenish lost engine coolant. Flares also work as emergency fire starters. When the alternator came off the engine block of my car one fine summer morning near the top of Mosca Pass, I was able to continue my trip by tensioning the alternator with a couple of elastic bungee cords. The jury-rigged maze of straps looked makeshift but it kept the water pump and alternator spinning for several hundred miles. In an emergency, the success of a repair job is measured not by its beauty or its conformity with established shop procedures, but by whether or not it works.

Factory jacks are usually adequate for tire changing on hard, level surfaces. But they can prove dangerous or useless under soft, sloping, or rutted conditions. Then, too, it is sometimes necessary to raise a vehicle at a point other than the one where the manufacturer's jack will work or raise the vehicle higher than the manufacturer intended. A heavy-duty accessory jack is worth its considerable weight in gold at these times. Equally valuable is a can of compressed air sealant; it can wholly eliminate the need to change a tire that has gone flat at an inconvenient time or place. And good tires, properly inflated for soft ground and with adequate tread, dramatically reduce the chance of tire problems in the first place. Good backcountry tires, incidentally, do not need the girth or tread pattern found on an earthmover. For most purposes in Colorado, a **high-quality snow tread pattern on a heavy-duty tire is wholly adequate and in some situations is clearly superior to the tractor-like tires used on many four-wheel-drive vehicles.**

Proper tire selection and maintenance is only the first part of a program of preparation for serious or sustained backcountry travel. Frequent or hard back road use creates higher than normal levels of stress on machinery and accelerates the rate of wear. Vehicles subjected to this kind of use should be equipped with heavy-duty components and receive much more frequent than normal maintenance and servicing.

Every motor vehicle, however, no matter how well equipped and maintained, has its limitations. There are places where it will not or should not go and things it cannot do. Exceeding these limits inevitably will damage equipment or cause bodily injury. Operating at the edge of these limits is an invitation to problems. The secret of safe, enjoyable backcountry travel is to know your own limits and the limitations of your equipment, then leave a sufficient margin of safety to accommodate the unexpected.

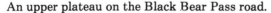

An upper plateau on the Black Bear Pass road.

Suggested Reading

Listed below are some of the standard reference works along with a few not so well known books on roads, trails, places, passes, people and events in the Colorado Rockies.

Akers, Carl. *Carl Akers' Colorado*, Old Army Press, Fort Collins, Colorado. 1975.

Athearn, Robert G. *Rebel of the Rockies: A History of the Denver and Rio Grande Western Railroad*, Yale University Press, New Haven and London. 1962. A carefully researched, nicely written and well illustrated history of that ambitious little railroad.

Beebe, Lucius and Clegg, Charles. *Narrow Gauge in the Rockies*, Howell-North, Berkeley, California. 1958. An older but well recognized study on the subject of mountain railroading.

Beebe, Lucius and Clegg, Charles. *Rio Grande: mainline of the Rockies*, Howell-North, Berkeley, California. 1962.

Borneman, Walter R. and Lampert, Lyndon J. *A Climbing Guide to Colorado's Fourteeners*, Pruett Publishing Company, Boulder, Colorado. 1978. An excellent guidebook and historical survey of the Fourteeners.

Brown, Robert L. *Jeep Trails to Colorado Ghost Towns*, The Caxton Printers Ltd., Caldwell, Idaho. 1963.

Brown, Robert L. *An Empire of Silver: a history of the San Juan Silver Rush*, The Caxton Printers Ltd., Caldwell, Idaho. 1965.

Brown, Robert L. *Ghost Towns of the Colorado Rocies*, The Caxton Printers, Caldwell, Idaho. 1968.

Brown, Robert L. *Colorado Ghost Towns, Past and Present*, The Caxton Printers Ltd., Caldwell, Idaho. 1972. Ranks along with his earlier ghost town books as a standard reference work on the subject.

Brown, Robert L. *Uphill Both Ways: hiking Colorado's High Country*, The Caxton Printers Ltd., Caldwell, Idaho. 1976. Includes descriptions of some interesting pass trails.

Chronic, John and Halka. *Prairie, Peak and Plateau*, Colorado Geological Society, Bulletin 32, Denver, Colorado. 1972. A well done introduction to Colorado's geology.

Eberhart, Perry. *Guide to the Colorado Ghost Towns and Mining Camps*, Sage Books, Denver, Colorado. 1969. Another of the standard reference works on the subject.

Eberhart, Perry. *Treasure Tales of the Colorado Rockies*, Sage Books, Chicago, Illinois. 1969.

Eberhart, Perry and Schmuck, Phillip. *The Fourteeners: Colorado's Great Mountains*, Swallow Press, Chicago, Illinois. 1970. Includes some very nice photography.

Edmondson, Clyde and Chloe. *Mountain Passes*, privately printed, Longmont, Colorado. 1963.

Eichler, George R. *Colorado Place Names: Communities, Counties, Peaks, Passes*, Johnson Publishing Company, Boulder, Colorado. 1977.

Goetzmann, William H. *Exploration and Empire: The Explorer and Scientist in the Winning of the West*, Alfred A. Knopf, New York, New York. 1966. A high quality historical study of the politics and personalities that drove the westward expansion.

Greever, William S. *The Bonanza West: The Story of the Western Mining Rushes, 1848-1900*, University of Oklahoma Press, Norman, Oklahoma. 1963. Another good historical study.

Hayden, F.V. *Annual Reports of the United States Geological and Geographical Survey*, Government Printing Office, Washington, D.C. Various dates. The volumes from 1873 to 1878 contain the majority of the Hayden Survey's findings on Colorado. For perspective, the Annual Reports should be read with Goetzmann's *Exploration and Empire* or Richard Bartlett's *Great Surveys of the American West*.

Hayden, F.V. *Geological and Geographical Atlas of Colorado and Portions of Adjacent Territory*, U.S. Department of the Interior, Washington, D.C., editions of 1877 and 1881. Modern maps are more accurate but much less beautiful than these finely done works of art.

Koch, Don. *An Endless Vista: Colorado's Recreational Lands*, Pruett Publishing Company, Boulder, Colorado. 1982.

Lavender, David. *David Lavender's Colorado*, Doubleday & Company, Garden City, New York. 1976. One of several books by this well known Colorado author.

Martin, Bob. *Hiking the Highest Passes*, Pruett Publishing Company, Boulder, Colorado. 1984. The definitive guide to hiking the high passes of Colorado.

Momaday, Scott N. *Colorado*, Rand McNally, Chicago, Illinois. 1973. Another well known book on the subject.

Norton, Boyd and Barbara. *Backroads of Colorado*, Rand McNally, Chicago, Illinois. 1978. Among the most recent and best of the tourguides.

O'Conner, Richard. *Iron Wheels and Broken Men: The Railroad Barons and the Plunder of the West*, G. P. Putnam's Sons, New York, New York. 1973. A lively and candid account of western railroading.

Ormes, Robert O. *Guide to the Colorado Mountains*, published by the author, Colorado Springs, Colorado. 1979. Now in its seventh edition, this is the hiking guide to own if you only plan to buy one.

Osterwald, Doris B. *Ticket to Toltec: A Mile By Mile Guide for the Cumbres and Toltec Scenic Railroad*, Western Guideways, Lakewood, Colorado. 1976. A lovingly detailed dissection of the Cumbres Pass railroad route. For perspective and background, this book should be read with a general study such as Beebe and Clegg's *Narrow Gauge in the Rockies* or Athearn's *Rebel of the Rockies*.

Sprague, Marshall. *The Great Gates: The Story of the Rocky Mountain Passes*, Little Brown and Company, Boston, Massachusetts. 1964. The definitive study of Rocky Mountain passes from Canada to New Mexico; it is exhaustively researched, well written and accurate. Contains good thumbnail pass sketches and best available bibliography.

Wolle, Muriel Sibell. *Stampede to Timberline: The Ghost Towns and Mining Camps of Colorado*, published by the author, Boulder, Colorado. No date.

Appendix C

A Tabulation of Colorado Backcountry Pass Roads: Organizational Sort

CPB No.	Pass Name	National Forest	County	Elevation (feet)
01	Buffalo	Routt	Jackson-Routt	10,180
02	Rollins	Roosevelt-Arapaho	Grand	11,671
03	Jones	Arapaho	Clear Creek-Grand	12,453
04	Stoney	Pike	Jefferson-Pike	8,560
05	Guanella	Arapaho	Clear Creek-Pike	11,669
06	Mosquito	Pike	Lake-Park	13,188
07	Weston	Pike-San Isabel	Lake-Park	11,921
08	Hayden	Rio Grande-San Isabel	Fremont-Saguache	10,709
09	Hermit	Rio Grande-San Isabel	Custer-Saguache	13,020
10	Music	Rio Grande-San Isabel	Custer-Saguache	11,380
11	Medano	Rio Grande-San Isabel	Huerfano-Saguache	9,950
12	Mosca	Rio Grande-San Isabel	Alamosa-Huerfano	9.713
13	Pass Creek	San Isabel	Costilla-Huerfano	9,400
14	La Veta	San Isabel	Costilla-Huerfano	9,382
15	Apishapa	San Isabel	Huerfano-Las Animas	11,248
16	Argentine	Arapaho-Pike	Clear Creek-Summit	13,207
17	Webster	Arapaho-Pike	Park-Summit	12,096
18	Georgia	Arapaho-Pike	Park-Summit	11,585
19	Boreas	Arapaho-Pike	Park-Summit	11,481
20	Shrine	Arapaho-White River	Eagle-Summit	11,089
21	Ute	Arapaho	Grand	9,524
22	Cochetopa	Gunnison-Rio Grande	Saguache	10,030
23	Marshall	Gunnison-San Isabel	Chaffee-Saguache	10,846
24	Old Monarch	Gunnison-San Isabel	Chaffee-Gunnison	11,375
25	Black Sage	Gunnison	Gunnison	9,745
26	Waunita	Gunnison	Gunnison	10,303
27	Cumberland	Gunnison	Gunnison	12,020
28	Tomichi	Gunnison	Gunnison	11,979
29	Hancock	Gunnison-San Isabel	Chaffee-Gunnison	12,140
30	Williams	Gunnison-San Isabel	Chaffee-Gunnison	11,762
31	Tincup	Gunnison-San Isabel	Chaffee-Gunnison	12,154
32	Cottonwood	Gunnison-San Isabel	Chaffee-Gunnison	12,126
33	Hagerman	San Isable-White River	Lake-Pitkin	11,925
34	Pearl	Gunnison-White River	Gunnison-Pitkin	12,705
35	Taylor	Gunnison-White River	Gunnison-Pitkin	11,928
36	Schofield	Gunnison	Gunnison-Pitkin	10,707
37	Ohio	Gunnison	Gunnison	10,003
38	Keebler	Gunnison	Gunnison	10,000
39	Cumbres	Rio Grande	Conejos	10,015
40	Stunner	Rio Grande	Conejos	10,541
41	Elwood	Rio Grande-San Juan	Mineral-Rio Grande	11,631
42	Los Piños	Gunnison	Hinsdale-Saguache	10,500
43	Owl Creek	Uncompahgre	Ouray-Gunnison	10,114
44	Stony	Rio Grande-Uncompahgre	Hinsdale-San Juan	12,588
45	Cinnamon	Uncompahgre	Hinsdale-Ouray	12,620
46	Yvonne	Uncompahgre	Hinsdale-Ouray	12,800
47	Engineer	Uncompahgre	Hinsdale-Ouray	12,750
48	Imogene	Uncompahgre	Ouray-San Miguel	13,114
49	Black Bear	Uncompahgre	San Juan-San Miguel	12,840
50	Ophir	San Juan-Uncompahgre	San Juan-San Miguel	11,789
51	Fall River	Rocky Mt. Nat. Park	Larimer	11,796
52	Browns	Pike	Park	11,372
53	Breakneck	Pike	Park	10,910
54	La Salle	Pike	Park	9,733
55	Ptarmigan	Arapaho-White River	Eagle-Summit	11,777
56	Red Cone	Arapaho-Pike	Park-Summit	12,600
57	Gunsight	Gunnison	Gunnison	12,090
58	Crooked Creek	White River	Eagle	10,020
59	West Cottonwood	White River	Eagle	8,280
60	Columbine	Uncompahgre	Montrose	9,120
61	Baxter	NA	Garfield	8,422
62	No Name	San Isabel	Huerfano	10,100

A Tabulation of Colorado Backcountry Pass Roads:
Alphabetical Sort

CPB No.	Pass Name	National Forest	County	Elevation (feet)
15	Apishapa	San Isabel	Huerfano-Las Animas	11,248
16	Argentine	Arapaho-Pike	Clear Creek-Summit	13,207
61	Baxter	NA	Garfield	8,422
49	Black Bear	Uncompahgre	San Juan-San Miguel	12,840
25	Black Sage	Gunnison	Gunnison	9,745
19	Boreas	Arapaho-Pike	Park-Summit	11,481
53	Breakneck	Pike	Park	10,910
52	Browns	Pike	Park	11,372
01	Buffalo	Routt	Jackson-Routt	10,180
45	Cinnamon	Uncompahgre	Hinsdale-Ouray	12,620
22	Cochetopa	Gunnison-Rio Grande	Saguache	10,030
60	Columbine	Uncompahgre	Montrose	9,120
32	Cottonwood	Gunnison-San Isabel	Chaffee-Gunnison	12,126
58	Crooked Creek	White River	Eagle	10,020
27	Cumberland	Gunnison	Gunnison	12,020
39	Cumbres	Rio Grande	Conejos	10,015
41	Elwood	Rio Grande-San Juan	Mineral-Rio Grande	11,631
47	Engineer	Uncompahgre	Hinsdale-Ouray	12,750
51	Fall River	Rocky Mt. Nat. Park	Larimer	11,796
18	Georgia	Arapaho-Pike	Park-Summit	11,585
05	Guanella	Arapaho	Clear Creek-Park	11,669
57	Gunsight	Gunnison	Gunnison	12,090
33	Hagerman	San Isabel-White River	Lake-Pitkin	11,925
29	Hancock	Gunnison-San Isabel	Chaffee-Gunnison	12,140
08	Hayden	Rio Grande-San Isabel	Fremont-Saguache	10,709
09	Hermit	Rio Grande-San Isabel	Custer-Saguache	13,020
48	Imogene	Uncompahgre	Ouray-San Miguel	13,114
03	Jones	Arapaho	Clear Creek-Grand	12,453
38	Keebler	Gunnison	Gunnison	10,000
14	La Veta	San Isabel	Costilla-Huerfano	9,382
54	La Salle	Pike	Park	9,733
42	Los Piños	Gunnison	Hinsdale-Saguache	10,500
23	Marshall	Gunnison-San Isabel	Chaffee-Saguache	10,846
11	Medano	Rio Grande-San Isabel	Huerfano-Saguache	9,950
12	Mosca	Rio Grande-San Isabel	Alamosa-Huerfano	9,713
06	Mosquito	Pike	Lake-Park	13,188
10	Music	Rio Grande-San Isabel	Custer-Saguache	11,380
62	No Name	San Isabel	Huerfano	10,100
37	Ohio	Gunnison	Gunnison	10,003
24	Old Monarch	Gunnison-San Isabel	Chaffee-Gunnison	11,375
50	Ophir	San Juan-Uncompahgre	San Juan-San Miguel	11,789
43	Owl Creek	Uncompahgre	Ouray-Gunnison	10,114
13	Pass Creek	San Isabel	Costilla-Huerfano	9,400
34	Pearl	Gunnison-White River	Gunnison-Pitkin	12,705
55	Ptarmigan	Arapaho-White River	Eagle-Summit	11,777
56	Red Cone	Arapaho-Pike	Park-Summit	12,600
02	Rollins	Roosevelt-Arapaho	Grand	11,671
36	Schofield	Gunnison	Gunnison-Pitkin	10,707
20	Shrine	Arapaho-White River	Eagle-Summit	11,089
04	Stoney	Pike	Jefferson-Pike	8,560
44	Stony	Rio Grande-Uncompahgre	Hinsdale-San Juan	12,588
40	Stunner	Rio Grande	Conejos	10,541
35	Taylor	Gunnison-White River	Gunnison-Pitkin	11,928
31	Tincup	Gunnison-San Isabel	Chaffee-Gunnison	12,154
28	Tomichi	Gunnison	Gunnison	11,979
21	Ute	Arapaho	Grand	9,524
26	Waunita	Gunnison	Gunnison	10,303
17	Webster	Arapaho-Pike	Park-Summit	12,096
59	West Cottonwood	White River	Eagle	8,280
07	Weston	Pike-San Isabel	Lake-Park	11,921
30	Williams	Gunnison-San Isabel	Chaffee-Gunnison	11,762
46	Yvonne	Uncompahgre	Hinsdale-Ouray	12,800

A Tabulation of Colorado Backcountry Pass Roads:
Elevation Sort

CPB No.	Pass Name	National Forest	County	Elevation (feet)
16	Argentine	Arapaho-Pike	Clear Creek-Summit	13,207
06	Mosquito	Pike	Lake-Park	13,188
48	Imogene	Uncompahgre	Ouray-San Miguel	13,114
09	Hermit	Rio Grande-San Isabel	Custer-Saguache	13,020
49	Black Bear	Uncompahgre	San Juan-San Miguel	12,840
46	Yvonne	Uncompahgre	Hinsdale-Ouray	12,800
47	Engineer	Uncompahgre	Hinsdale-Ouray	12,750
34	Pearl	Gunnison-White River	Gunnison-Pitkin	12,705
45	Cinnamon	Uncompahgre	Hinsdale-Ouray	12,620
56	Red Cone	Arapaho-Pike	Park-Summit	12,600
44	Stony	Rio Grande-Uncompahgre	Hinsdale-San Juan	12,588
03	Jones	Arapaho	Clear Creek-Grand	12,453
31	Tincup	Gunnison-San Isabel	Chaffee-Gunnison	12,154
29	Hancock	Gunnison-San Isabel	Chaffee-Gunnison	12,140
32	Cottonwood	Gunnison-San Isabel	Chaffee-Gunnison	12,126
17	Webster	Arapaho-Pike	Park-Summit	12,096
57	Gunsight	Gunnison	Gunnison	12,090
27	Cumberland	Gunnison	Gunnison	12,020
28	Tomichi	Gunnison	Gunnison	11,979
35	Taylor	Gunnison-White River	Gunnison-Pitkin	11,928
33	Hagerman	San Isabel-White River	Lake-Pitkin	11,925
07	Weston	Pike-San Isabel	Lake-Park	11,921
51	Fall River	Rocky Mt. Nat. Park	Larimer	11,796
50	Ophir	San Juan-Uncompahgre	San Juan-San Miguel	11,789
55	Ptarmigan	Arapaho-White River	Eagle-Summit	11,777
30	Williams	Gunnison-San Isabel	Chaffee-Gunnison	11,762
02	Rollins	Roosevelt-Arapaho	Grand	11,671
05	Guanella	Arapaho	Clear Creek-Park	11,669
41	Elwood	Rio Grande-San Juan	Mineral-Rio Grande	11,631
18	Georgia	Arapaho-Pike	Park-Summit	11,585
19	Boreas	Arapaho-Pike	Park-Summit	11,481
10	Music	Rio Grande-San Isabel	Custer-Saguache	11,380
24	Old Monarch	Gunnison-San Isabel	Chaffee-Gunnison	11,375
52	Browns	Pike	Park	11,372
15	Apishapa	San Isabel	Huerfano-Las Animas	11,248
20	Shrine	Arapaho-White River	Eagle-Summit	11,089
53	Breakneck	Pike	Park	10,910
23	Marshall	Gunnison-San Isabel	Chaffee-Saguache	10,846
08	Hayden	Rio Grande-San Isabel	Fremont-Saguache	10,709
36	Schofield	Gunnison	Gunnison-Pitkin	10,707
40	Stunner	Rio Grande	Conejos	10,541
42	Los Piños	Gunnison	Hinsdale-Saguache	10,500
26	Waunita	Gunnison	Gunnison	10,303
01	Buffalo	Routt	Jackson-Routt	10,180
43	Owl Creek	Uncompahgre	Ouray-Gunnison	10,114
62	No Name	San Isabel	Huerfano	10,100
22	Cochetopa	Gunnison-Rio Grande	Saguache	10,030
58	Crooked Creek	White River	Eagle	10,020
39	Cumbres	Rio Grande	Conejos	10,015
37	Ohio	Gunnison	Gunnison	10,003
38	Keebler	Gunnison	Gunnison	10,000
11	Medano	Rio Grande-San Isabel	Huerfano-Saguache	9,950
25	Black Sage	Gunnison	Gunnison	9,745
54	La Salle	Pike	Park	9,733
12	Mosca	Rio Grande-San Isabel	Alamosa-Huerfano	9,713
21	Ute	Arapaho	Grand	9,524
13	Pass Creek	San Isabel	Costilla-Huerfano	9,400
14	La Veta	San Isabel	Costilla-Huerfano	9,382
60	Columbine	Uncompahgre	Montrose	9,120
04	Stoney	Pike	Jefferson-Pike	8,560
61	Baxter	NA	Garfield	8,422
59	West Cottonwood	White River	Eagle	8,280

Index of Passes

About the Author

Don Koch, born in Pittsburgh, Pennsylvania, was educated at the Nichols School, Brandeis University, Princeton University and the University of Colorado. An avid sports enthusiast and owner of a consulting firm that provides planning and other services for a variety of clients, he has traveled extensively throughout the West. His writings include three books, more than forty articles, essays and reviews and numerous technical publications and documents on land use and environmental matters, economic planning research, fiscal impact analysis and human resource development.